# Important

## How to Use the Reflector

With the enclosed sheet of reflecting plastic you can correct the distorted pictures in the Game Section of this book—pages 137–176—and watch small marvels of painting emerge from the confusion of shapes and colors.

1     Roll the silver sheet into a cylinder about an inch in diameter.

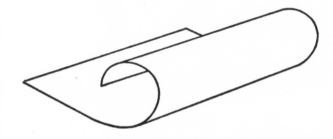

2     Holding the cylinder together firmly, look at one of the pictures. It will be easier to manipulate the cylinder if you tape the edges together. We suggest that you unroll the cylinder after use in order to keep it from cracking or creasing.

3     In each picture in the Game Section there is a circle or a square that indicates where the reflecting cylinder should be placed.

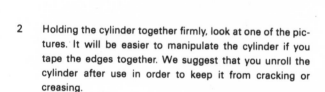

4     If you have placed the cylinder correctly on the page, the concealed picture will become clearly visible.

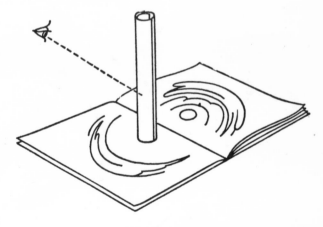

The "game" is in finding the correct angle from which each picture should be observed. Your eye should always be somewhat higher than the cylinder, as it will be if you sit at a table and place the open book in front of you.

Experiment with the cylinder! See how the reflected pictures change when you alter its circumference. Several anamorphoses are more clearly seen when the diameter of the cylinder is about two to two-and-a-half inches.

# HIDDEN IMAGES

# HIDDEN IMAGES

## Games of Perception
## Anamorphic Art · Illusion

### FROM THE RENAISSANCE TO THE PRESENT

TEXT BY
**Fred Leeman**

CONCEPT, PRODUCTION, and PHOTOGRAPHS BY
**Joost Elffers and Mike Schuyt**

TRANSLATION BY
**Ellyn Childs Allison AND Margaret L. Kaplan**

**Harry N. Abrams, Inc., Publishers, New York**

*Photographs are by Michael Schuyt except for the following, which were kindly supplied by the persons or institutions named:*

Alinari, Florence: 6, 8–12, 20, 160; Apolloni, Rome: 55–58, 153–55; J. Baltrušaitis, Paris: 45; Bibliothèque Nationale, Paris: 7; Galerie Art & Project, Amsterdam: 123; Historisches Museum, Basel: 137-38; National Gallery, London: 2, 67, 75; Nationalmuseum, Copenhagen: 76, 82, 139; Science Museum, London: 98–99; Universitätsbibliothek, Leiden: 46

**Library of Congress Cataloging in Publication Data**

Leeman, Fred.
Hidden images: games of perception, anamorphic art, illusion

   German translation has title: Anamorphosen.
   1. Visual perception. 2. Optical illusions.
3. Perspective. I. Elffers, Joost. II. Schuyt,
Michael. III. Title.
N7430.5.L4313      709      76-3736
ISBN 0-8109-9019-9

Library of Congress Catalogue Card Number: 76-3736
Copyright © 1975 by Verlag M. DuMont Schauberg, Cologne
Published in 1976 by Harry N. Abrams, Incorporated, New York
Printed and bound in U.S.A.

# Contents

# Introduction

The system of central perspective not only rationalizes the relationship between objects within a picture, but also establishes a relationship between the viewer and the represented images. Anamorphoses are an extreme example of this subjectivization of the viewing process. The observer is first deceived by a barely recognizable image, and is then directed to a viewpoint dictated by the formal construction of the painting. Indeed, the etymological origin of the word —from the Greek *ana* (again), *morphē* (shape)—indicates that the spectator must play a part and re-form the picture himself. In this respect the anamorphosis is not a unique phenomenon, of course. Similar characteristics can be found in illusionistic wall and ceiling painting, and in the use of accelerated and retarded perspective in architecture, urban design, and theatrical scenery. A typically Dutch application of this principle is the perspective cabinet or "perspektyfkas."

Since perspective anamorphosis is also an offshoot of the central perspective system in structure, we will briefly examine the history of its discovery and the method by which it is constructed. We will also examine other closely related variants and special applications, such as illusionistic and *quadratura* painting. The relationship between perspective anamorphoses and various kinds of accelerated perspective extends beyond their comparative constructions. All these techniques are intended to invoke a realistic visual effect disassociated from the actual concrete, material nature of the object.

The seventeenth and eighteenth centuries were the golden age of anamorphosis. Illustrative examples from books, paintings, and prints—including much hitherto unpublished material—give an idea of how many imaginative variations on a long-familiar theme were conceived in this period. In the nineteenth century, anamorphoses were relegated to children's rooms and—as exercises—to the art schools. The search for the basis of anamorphic effect in the psychology of perception is characteristic of the attitudes of the twentieth century and—once clarified and defined—the phenomenon seems to have been consigned to the archives.

The places where anamorphoses can be found today give an indication of their obscure and equivocal position. Museums of natural history regard them as mere diversions in the field of optics. In the art museums they tend to be overlooked because of their frequently undistinguished artistic quality.

Yet anamorphic art has crept back in—in the art of Dutch artist Jan Dibbets, for example. Here, anamorphosis appears to have reached a status it never achieved earlier: as full-scale fine art. In light of this, perhaps we should rethink our interpretations of what fine art encompassed in the sixteenth and seventeenth centuries.

Jurgis Baltrušaitis has revived interest in the study of anamorphic art, and all subsequent scholarship must remain heavily in his debt. His volume *Anamorphoses* is the only work that deals exclusively with this subject, and has laid the foundation for all further studies. It was first published in France in 1955 by Olivier Perrin Éditeur; Perrin brought out a new, much enlarged and revised edition in 1969,which is being published in the United States by Harry N. Abrams (English translation copyright © Chadwyck-Healey Ltd., Cambridge, England).The illustrative material and the historical and technical development in the present volume relating to anamorphic images are derived from Baltrušaitis's work and from his personal assistance.

A number of the works illustrated in the present volume have never been published before. The majority were photographed especially for this book.The text explores the ways in which perspective can be used to deceive the human eye, and at the end there is a Game Section in which—with the enclosed sheet of reflecting plastic—you can explore the world of cylinder anamorphoses for yourself.

9

# 1. The First Anamorphoses

Leonardo da Vinci: Codex Atlanticus

The Biblioteca Ambrosiana in Milan has a large collection of Leonardo da Vinci's notes and drawings, pasted on 393 album pages by the sculptor Pompeo Leoni, the man who owned them about 1600. On folio 35 verso *a* of this volume, now called the Codex Atlanticus, are two extremely elongated sketches[1] (Fig. 1).

The distortion of both sketches makes the images—a baby's head and an eye—difficult to recognize. Nevertheless, the distortion follows a regular progression, increasing from right to left. In the sketch of the eye, one can distinguish vertical lines

*Fig. 1* Leonardo da Vinci. Anamorphic sketches of a child's head and an eye, Codex Atlanticus, fol. 35 verso *a*. c.1485. Biblioteca Ambrosiana, Milan

These hesitant distorted drawings are the first anamorphoses we know of. When they are viewed from a sharp angle at the righthand side of the page, the pictures regain their normal proportions and also seem to rise and float free above the paper.

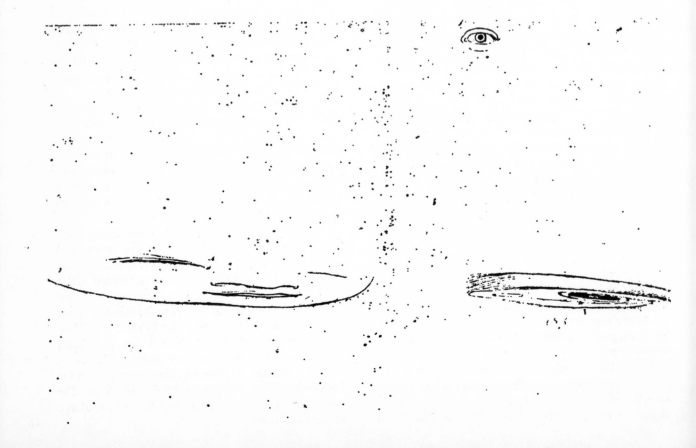

whose distance from each other also increases. In fact, the original seems to be covered with a network of fine lines, drawn with a metal point.[2] On the basis of these lines, we can conclude that both sketches are so constructed that they must be looked at from a sharp angle at the right. When you close one eye and, with the other, look at the picture from a specific point about an inch from the right edge of the paper, the distortion corrects itself and the intervals between the vertical lines appear to be the same. Moreover, the sketches now seem to disengage themselves from the background and float in space. Above, as a kind of check, Leonardo has sketched an undistorted eye. Unfortunately, the notes that accompany them have no bearing on these unusual sketches.

From indirect sources we can infer that these sketches do not represent an isolated, casual discovery by Leonardo. In his treatise of 1584 on painting, the art theoretician and painter Giovanni Paolo Lomazzo describes in minute detail a "method of making an inverted perspective that looks correct when it is observed through a single peephole."[3] We will consider the instructions he gives later. At this point, it is the examples he offers that are particularly interesting.

"I have seen such a one," he writes, "by Gaudentio [Gaudenzio], a Christ in profile, whose hair resembles the waves of the sea, but when one approached the little hole—there appeared a very beautiful head of Christ.[4] Francesco Melzi related that in the same fashion Leonardo made a dragon that fought with a lion—a wonder to behold.[5] He similarly constructed the horses that he gave to Francis I, king of France. This same method was very cleverly employed by Girolamo Ficino when drawing horses."

Apparently the technique was fairly well known, particularly in northern Italy. A peephole helped give the correct position of the eye.

This is, moreover, not the only mention of a "fight between a dragon and lion" by Leonardo. In another passage, Lomazzo informs us that he owns a drawing on the same subject by Leonardo, of which he was "very proud."[6] Two drawings exist, either of which might have been the one in Lomazzo's possession.

There also exists an engraving, which has been attributed to Zoan Andrea, a copy of a design of Leonardo's on the same theme.[7] It may be interpreted as an allegory of a dispute between Milan and Venice, whose symbols are dragon and lion.[8]

Dating the first sketches is extremely difficult. The date of one drawing of the dragon and the lion may be established at about 1478, on the basis of another sketch on the same sheet. Since the child's head and

the eye have a very experimental character, they must have been done before this year. This dating does not, of course, take into account a possible later "distortion" of the dragon and the lion. The horses for Francis I that Lomazzo also mentions were very probably made when Leonardo was in France—that is, after 1516.[9]

Erhard Schön

A very large woodcut by Erhard Schön, follower of Albrecht Dürer and graphic artist of Nuremberg, seems at first glance to be composed of unrecognizable, bizarre forms intermingled with a few landscape fragments (Fig. 2). However, when we look at this woodcut alternately from left and right at a sharp angle, four portraits emerge from the chaos. Starting from the top, one sees (looking from the left) Emperor Charles V, enclosed in a simple landscape showing a city, soldiers, and beasts of burden. Next, viewed from the right, his brother Ferdinand of Austria appears, beside a view of Vienna under siege by the Turks. Below, the beard of Pope Paul III flows out in waves, over which a ship sails. On the other side of the pope, a Turkish rider flees before the wrath of God. Last of the four is King Francis I. His landscape includes two crosses marking graves. Below, the print terminates with a landscape in which a figure, probably again Francis I, is seen standing, as a Turkish rider and camel driver approach him.

Probably Schön used the same method of construction for his woodcut as did Leonardo for his sketches. Schön's virtuoso handling of line, however, attests a complete mastery of the technique. The way in which the mingled forms in the landscapes are handled—particularly in the portrait of Paul III—is reminiscent of Lomazzo's description of the head of Christ by Gaudenzio Ferrari.

The historical details in the print make dating possible. Vienna was besieged in 1529. The storm with which God repels the Turkish rider is probably an allusion to the incessant downpours that forced Sultan Suleiman II to lift the siege on October 16 of that year. A key to the date as well as to the meaning of the picture lies in the landscape under Francis I. In 1534, Francis negotiated with Suleiman for a military alliance and a trade agreement against Charles V. This un-Christian behavior—dealing secretly with the Turks—provoked an uproar in Christendom. The angel of the Last Judgment at the left can be read as a warning to Francis.

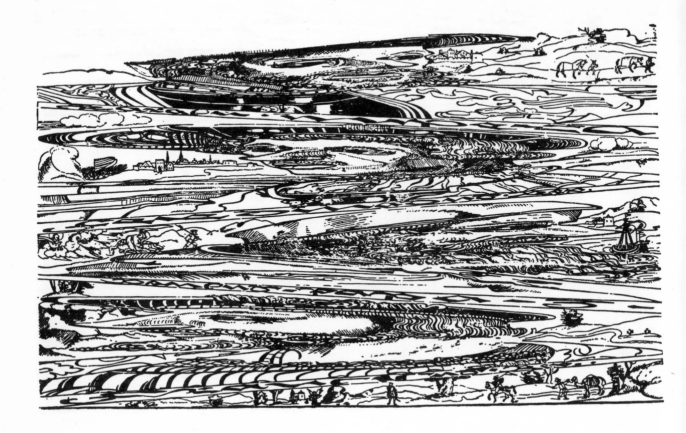

*Fig. 2* Erhard Schön. Picture puzzle: *Portraits of Charles V, Ferdinand of Austria, Pope Paul III, and Francis I.* c.1535. Woodcut, 17⅜ x 29½" (44 x 75 cm)

Unrecognizably distorted and completely hidden in landscapes, four of the leading political figures of their time are here united by Dürer's pupil. Viewed alternately from left and right, the four likenesses, which closely resemble those in other portraits, emerge from the confusion of lines. The virtuosity with which the anamorphic process is used indicates that the experimental phase of this technique is over. Indeed, this anamorphosis verges on caricature.

*Fig. 3* Jacobus Typotius, *Symbola . . .* (Prague, 1604; facsimile ed., Graz, 1973), illus. 23. A motto of King Francis I

Fig. 4 Erhard Schön. Picture puzzle: *What Do You See?* ("Was siehst du?"). 1538. Woodcut printed and signed by Stefan Hamer of Nuremberg

This type of witty representation proves to be an ever-recurring one. The analogy between the man relieving himself and the whale that spat out Jonah is a truly original interpretation of this Biblical event.

Fig. 5 Erhard Schön. Picture puzzle: *Out, You Old Fool* ("Aus, du alter Tor"). c. 1535. Woodcut

Anamorphoses supplied an ideal means of camouflaging themes that contained double meanings. The distorted representation shows the continuation of the story that could already be guessed at in the normal rendering: The role of the graybeard is played out. The stag harried into the net in the hunting scene at the picture's upper border symbolizes the main theme.

Hans Holbein: *The Ambassadors*

Probably the best-known example of such singular distortion is Holbein's double portrait *The Ambassadors* (Plates 2, 3). To left and right of a bookshelf filled with volumes and musical and mathematical instruments stand Jean de Dinteville, the ambassador of the French king to the English court, and his friend Georges de Selve.[10]

The exceptional precision with which the various complicated geometrical forms are re-created, the virtuoso rendering of textures and substances, and the large format (the painting measures more than six feet on each side) give the picture the aspect of a *trompe l'oeil*. Its composition is such that the beholder feels he is standing in the same room with the two men.

In a prominent positionin this looking-glass world, however, is a startling object. At the feet of the ambassador and his friend is something very difficult to interpret, until, as before, you look along the long axis of the form, at eye level, close to the wall against which the painting hangs; then you see at once that it is a skull.

Jurgis Baltrušaitis has drawn attention to the fact that this "discovery" puts the whole picture in another light.[11] It has also been suggested that this skull, this "hollow bone" (in German, "hohle Bein") is a rebus, a pictorial pun on the name of the artist. This interpretation is not so trite as it might seem at first,[12] for puns and word games were a regular component of contemporary humor. It was the custom of this period to attach as many meanings to things as possible. This need not be the only explanation for the appearance of the skull in this place, however. Also the appearance of a skull *in this form* is not explained.

A green damask curtain serves as the background of the painting, running parallel to the picture plane. The pictorial stage is bounded by it; there, the artificial space ends and flows into the surface of the picture. But a glance at the upper left indicates that behind the curtain lies a different world. A corner of the hanging is turned back and reveals a crucifix.

The floor is mosaic of the style known as Cosmati work, and the pattern is eccentrically placed with regard to the central vertical axis of the picture. With a few deviations, it is a representation of the pavement of the choir in Westminster Abbey.

The shelves supporting the still-life arrangements are also parallel to the picture plane; they are, however, slightly off center. On the shelves are objects, each one of which challenged the artist's ability to reproduce it in proper perspective and naturally lit. On the lower shelf are earthly things, as is indicated by the terrestrial globe at the left, which contrasts clearly with the globe of the heavens on the upper shelf. The lute is a favorite motif in tour-de-force renderings of perspective effects; it also embodies, with the flutes and the music book, the most evanescent of all the arts. The lute's broken string can be understood as a representation of discord (as an emblem, the lute stands for *concordia*). The broken string might, in this light, symbolize the withdrawal of Milan from the alliance that England, France, and the Italian principalities had made against Charles V.

On the upper shelf, the heavenly realm, denoted by the globe of the heavens, is represented by a profusion of instruments for determining the position of the stars and regulating time. Possibly linked to this still life is a device of Francis I, which makes incontrovertible allusion to another world (Fig. 3). It shows a heavenly and an earthly globe, accompanied by the motto "Unus non Sufficit Orbis" (One World Is Not Enough).

The two ambassadors lean on the upper shelf. Jean de Dinteville wears a splendid costume; he stands slightly to the front of the picture as estimable representative of the active life, a participant in worldly affairs. His hand rests on his dagger. On the richly decorated scabbard is engraved his age: twenty-nine years. His cap is decorated with a brooch, engraved with a death's-head on a shield. Rendering the inscription on it must have exceeded even the ability of Holbein. This device has an evident relationship with the other death's-head on the floor.

On the right, slightly to the rear, is Georges de Selve, representing the contemplative life. He wears his bishop's robes. His right arm rests on a book (the Bible, perhaps), on which his age is disclosed as twenty-five years.

All these allusions to the relativity and transience of life have, paradoxically, been made timeless in the art of the painter. The skull expresses more than this. It is not only an enlarged version of De Dinteville's device or a play on words. It brings together the most technically brilliant forms of painterly illusion and is a most eloquent example of the *relativity* of the painterly procedure.

Holbein signed the painting and dated it 1533.

These three examples indicate the remarkable development of distorted perspective. Leonardo's sketches were the first hesitant experiments, Schön's woodcut a dazzling example in a caricaturistic, politicized, satirical vein. In Holbein's *Ambassadors* the technique creates an artistic symbol of the relativity of life.

These different examples prompt many questions. It is clear that departures from perspective norms can be made only in a milieu in which these norms are common property. This peculiar type of construction can only be truly perceived against a background of "normal" perspective.

Although we may establish a connection between perspectival distortion and central perspective, we still have no answer to the question in what context and for what sorts of objects each is most often used. This aspect of our investigation, the meaning of choice of form, was briefly touched upon and will be so again.

Often artists choose the technique of anamorphosis for its covert nature. What must be kept secret is often obscene or erotic. This theme, too, was taken up at an early stage. Two more anamorphic pictures by Erhard Schön are known. One, bearing the name and city of residence of Stefan Hamer, is dated 1538 (Fig. 4). Here, too, Schön took pains to make a smooth transition between the main picture and the small scenes surrounding it. These bear a formal relationship and also contribute to the main theme.

In the distortion, one sees a squatting man relieving himself. Behind him, a ram is about to attack. The man's hat turns into a ship in the undistorted upper part of the picture, and in it men are hunting a sea monster, Jonah's whale. At upper left we see the whale spitting Jonah out on land—right over the squatting man—in an utterly irreverent analogy. The woodcut bears the inscription, "What do you see?"

The other picture dexterously exploits a sequence of perceptual images (Fig. 5). At left one sees, in normal representation, a girl tempting an old man and stealing his money, which she gives to a young man. A fool peers around the corner. The right half of the picture is anamorphic and can be viewed from the normal half of the illustration through a little "window." The old man has served his purpose, and the young pair exchange caresses. This anamorphosis is bordered by little pictures of a merry group in a boat and, above, by a deer hunt. The stag, driven toward a net, is an allusion to the fate of the old man. The caption reads, "OUT, YOU OLD FOOL."

Notes

1 On Leonardo and anamorphosis, see F. S. Bassoli, "Leonardo da Vinci e l'invenzione delle anamorfosi," *Atti della Società dei Naturalisti e Matematici di Modena* 69 (ser. 6, no. 16, 1938): 61–67; C. Pedretti, *Studio Vinciani* (Geneva, 1957), pp. 68–76.

2 C. Pedretti, *op. cit.*, p. 73.

3 Giovanni Paolo Lomazzo, *Trattato dell'arte della pittura. . . .* (Rome, 1844), vol. 2, pp. 174–75.

4 Gaudenzio Ferrari (c. 1475–1546), a Piedmontese painter who concerned himself with the combination of frescoes and painted lifesize terra-cotta figures.

5 Francesco Melzi, Leonardo's pupil and heir to his manuscripts.

6 C. Pedretti, *op. cit.*, p. 74.

7 See A. M. Hind, *Early Italian Engraving* (London, 1938–48), vol. 6, no. 579.

8 There exists a drawing by Jacopo Bellini of a man, with a lion painted on his shield, who fights a dragon.

9 C. Pedretti, *op. cit.*, p. 75.

10 For biographical information about the people pictured, see M. F. S. Hervey, *Holbein's Ambassadors* (London, 1900).

11 J. Baltrušaitis, *Anamorphoses* (Paris, 1969), Chapter 7.

12 E. Panofsky, *Galileo as a Critic of the Arts* (The Hague, 1954), p. 14.

*To the plates on pages 17–20*

1   William Scrots. *Portrait of Edward VI*. 1546. Oil on panel, 16¾ x 63″ (42.5 x 160 cm). National Portrait Gallery, London

    Under the influence of Holbein, William Scrots used perspective means convincingly. There is a hollow in the frame through which one can view the work from the correct angle. The reproduction below shows the painting from this correct viewpoint, the one above as it appears viewed in the ordinary fashion.

2   Hans Holbein the Younger. *The Ambassadors*. 1533. Oil on panel, 81½ x 82½″ (206 x 209.5 cm). National Gallery, London

    When Holbein painted this lifesize double portrait of Jean de Dinteville, the French ambassador, and his friend, Bishop Georges de Selve, in England, he surrounded them with attributes that could be interpreted in various ways. The highly detailed still lifes in the center show the interests of both friends, yet at the same time refer to the transitory nature of human endeavors. The crucifix just barely visible beyond the drapery at upper left sustains this theme. The elongated form in the lower foreground pierces the painterly illusion and makes it relative. For when one looks at it from above at the right, it is seen to be a skull.

3   Detail of Plate 2. The skull seen from the upper right

4   Anonymous south German. Perspective anamorphosis: *Saint Peter and Saint Paul; Christ and the Angel in Gethsemane; Veronica's Veil; Madonna and Child; Saint Francis of Assisi Receiving the Stigmata*. c. 1550. Oil on panel, 21¼ x 33⅞″ (54 x 86 cm). Collection Bazzi, Milan

    The themes, artfully camouflaged as landscape, must be viewed from the side. For this purpose there are small peepholes in the frame.

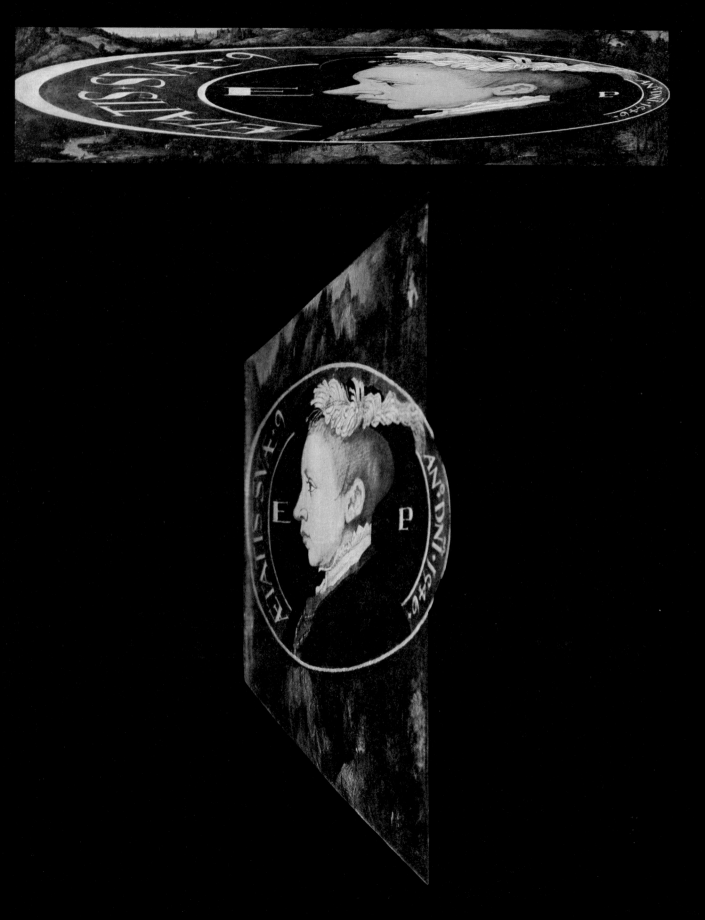

2

3 ▷

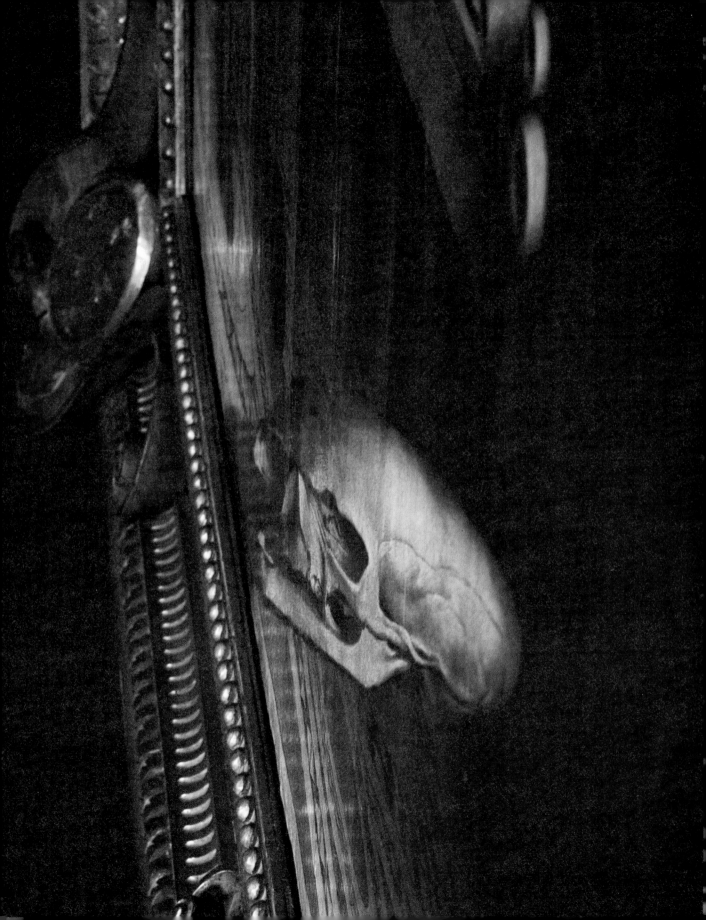

4

# 2. The Discovery of Perspective

The sculptor Pomponio Gaurico described the implications of the discovery of perspective in clear and distinctive fashion. In his treatise of 1504, *De Sculptura*, he remarks: "Each body in whatever position it is, finds itself necessarily in one or another location. Since this is so, we must consider which was there first. And inasmuch as it is inevitable that the location was there before the object placed on it, it is the location that must be constructed first."[1] With this observation, which opens his chapter on perspective, Gaurico summarized the meaning of the development in the representation of space that had begun more than eighty years earlier. At the beginning of this development was the discovery of perspective construction. It was the product of two disciplines—the study of optics and practical experimentation by painters in their studios.

*Fig. 6* These drawings show how Brunelleschi constructed his painting of the Baptistery in Florence and how it should be observed: a) 1 Baptistery 2 Cathedral 3 Observation point; b) 1 Mirror 2 Picture

Filippo Brunelleschi

About 1485 an anonymous author, most probably Antonio Manetti, wrote a biography of the Florentine architect and sculptor Filippo Brunelleschi, who had died in 1446. In one passage that is particularly interesting from our point of view, Manetti describes two works by Brunelleschi, which he remarks he has himself held in his hand.[2]

The first was a small panel painting about a foot square, a view of the Baptistery in Florence from the central door of the cathedral (Fig. 6). This picture had to be observed in a particular way: One had to stand exactly where the artist had stood when he painted his subject—that is, almost six feet inside the entrance of the church. A peephole had been cut in the center of the picture, and the viewer had to look through it from

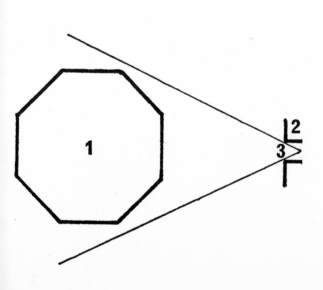

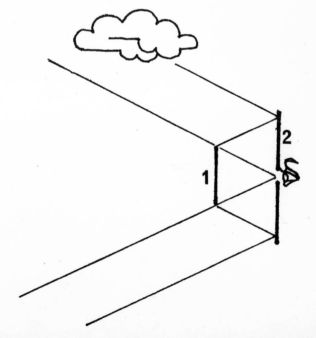

the back of the picture. Gazing through the hole, he would see the cathedral square and the Baptistery just as Brunelleschi had painted them. Then, holding up a mirror, he could look through the peephole and this time see the front of the painting, which coincided exactly with the actual view of the square. In order to enhance the effect, the sky was not painted in on the panel; instead, a layer of silver reflected the real sky. "And so," as Manetti writes, "the clouds that one saw in the silver moved with the wind when it blew."

The other painting described by Manetti showed a view of the Palazzo Vecchio. One did not have to look at this one with the aid of a mirror; one simply looked at it from the front in the normal way. But, in this case, the sky was cut away. When the viewer took the correct position, the contours of the picture hid the real buildings that rose against the sky behind it.

In such spectacular fashion Brunelleschi emphasized the illusionistic character of his invention. With this perspective system it was possible to create a facsimile of visual reality on a flat surface. His method—particularly in the first picture—illustrates several important conditions that must be met in creating illusions of this type. In the first picture, the peephole fixed the eye of the beholder exactly where the vanishing point of the artist's perspective construction lay. Moreover, the apparent distance between the eye of the viewer and the mirrored image was predetermined. In this case it was naturally double the distance between the mirror and the picture. The establishment of these two points symbolizes an important shift in the relation between the viewer, reality, and the representation. What the individual person sees through a peephole will determine its representation. The mutual relationships between the objects that he observes, their apparent sizes, and their distance can be shown on a flat surface. When, with the aid of a mirror, he keeps the distance to this flat surface exact, he can control all this himself and reconstruct his observation.

The dating of the pictures, both lost today, ranges from 1418 to 1425.

## Leonbattista Alberti

The art theorist Leonbattista Alberti, in his treatise *De Pictura* of 1435, offered the first formal description of the central perspective system that Brunelleschi had recommended in such a direct and easy-to-follow manner.[3]

Alberti begins by comparing the surface of a picture to an open window through which one sees what one wants to paint. What one sees is contained in an imaginary pyramid whose apex lies in the observer's eye (Fig. 7). The picture plane is a cross section through the pyramid, as shown by the arrow. The apparent distance of objects—for example, the two verticals behind the arrow—is governed by the visual angle of the viewer. As an example of a surface which he wishes to show in perspective, Alberti offers a pavement that is divided, like a chessboard, into squares. First, the sides of the squares are marked off on the bottom edge of the picture. These points are then connected by straight lines with the vanishing point, which is located where the central axis of the visual pyramid cuts the picture (Fig. 8, right). Such a construction, with a vanishing point for lines that are parallel not to the picture plane but to each other, was already known to the Sienese painter Ambrogio Lorenzetti in the fourteenth century. Alberti's contribution here is the connection he makes with the position of the viewer.

Now, how are the transversals—the parallel horizontal lines—of a chessboard receding into the distance to be established? To do this, Alberti used an auxiliary diagram (Fig. 8, far left). We must look at the picture and the visual pyramid from the side: The transversals of the chessboard would look from this viewpoint like a series of dots, the distances between which would be equal to those between the lines to the vanishing point at the bottom of the first drawing in Fig. 8. So, if we connect a similarly placed series of points on the new groundline with the new viewpoint, which is at the same height as is the vanishing point, we get, on the vertical line that in this diagram represents the picture plane, a series of points of intersection. These divisions can then be joined by lines to the first drawing (Fig. 8, center) and they determine how the rows of squares should recede in depth. The results can be counterproved by drawing diagonal lines through the intersection points. When spatial relations have been established in this fashion, we can begin to draw in the figures and objects.

This projection of space on a flat surface makes an impression of extreme objectivity; nevertheless, certain assumptions have been made. Thus, the vanishing point only controls horizontal planes. Vertical ones remain parallel. That this is by no means the case in actuality is known to anyone who has taken a photograph of a church tower. Moreover, according to Alberti's system, lines running parallel to the cross section through the visual pyramid remain parallel, whereas in theory their separation becomes larger to left and right of the line of sight. These phenomena,

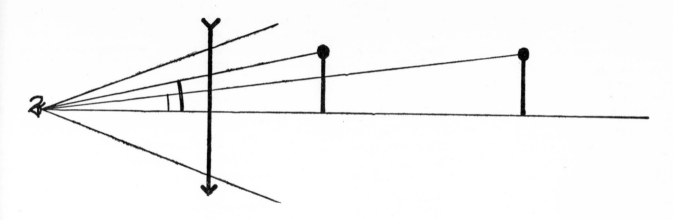

*Fig. 7*  Leonbattista  Alberti. Visual pyramid.

*Fig. 8*  Leonbattista  Alberti. Perspective constructions

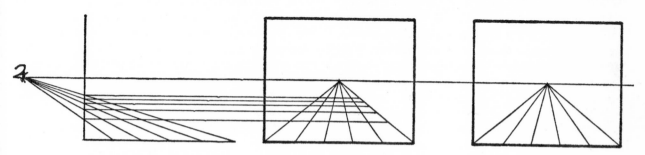

which were already known to theoreticians of optics in ancient times and which also had been taken into account by students in the Middle Ages, were to lead to a new evaluation of Alberti's construction toward the end of the fifteenth century.


Piero della Francesca

In his book *De Prospectiva Pingendi* (*On Painting in Perspective*) the painter and mathematician Piero della Francesca gives a full account of how ground plans must be altered in perspective construction. With his method it is possible to work into a picture buildings for which one has the exact measurements. A well-known painting by Piero, *The Flagellation of Christ*, shows a space constructed in such a fashion (Plate 5).

The regular division of the pavement shows the skeleton of his construction. It is so precisely executed that we today can make a ground plan of the space shown in the painting (Fig. 9). The panel, which is only 23 by 32 inches in size, depicts an area that is a good 46 feet deep, measured to the back wall. One can also reconstruct how the whole would look from the side. Not long ago, the fascinating theory was proposed that the measurements of this building correspond to those of a building that actually existed in Jerusalem—and was presumed to be the palace of Pontius Pilate.[4]

Piero's method also made it possible to draw imaginary city views from a building constructed according to his rules. In this way, a viewer could form an idea of a city in which the ideals of Renaissance architecture were embodied.

But even at a very early stage, variations of these constructions in "normal" perspective were proposed that have a distinct bearing on our particular interest.


Curved Perspective

North of the Alps, painters used convex mirrors when sketching landscapes, thereby enlarging their angle of

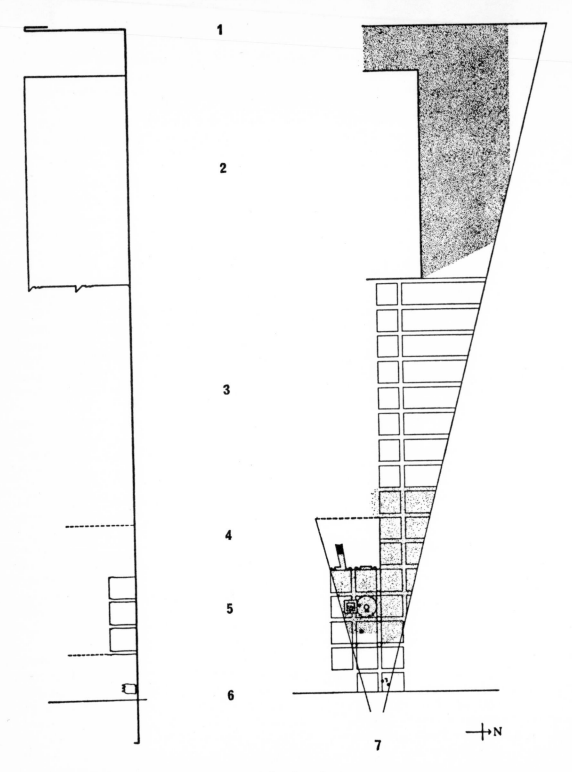

1

2

3

4

5

6

7

→N

*Fig. 9* Reconstruction of the groundplan and elevation of *The Flagellation of Christ* by Piero della Francesca (after Lavin). See Plate 5
1 Wall  2 Second building in the background  3 Open area  4 Palace  5 Judgment hall  6 Picture plane  7 Observation point

vision considerably. When this aid is used for interior views, a distortion can be clearly observed. This effect is particularly noticeable in the church interiors of the Swiss artist Conrad Witz (Plate 6).

The painter Jean Fouquet traveled in 1445 from Burgundy to Italy. In the work he executed after his return—the Book of Hours of Etienne Chevalier—are reflected many points of influence from the Renaissance. Several architectural elements are reminiscent of Alberti, and the perspective also seems Italian. In several miniatures, however, Fouquet still seems to have used the convex mirror. In the *Annunciation of the Death of the Virgin*, the curved lines of the raftered ceiling and patterned floor are very noticeable. Nonlinear perspective plays an even more important role in another miniature, representing the arrival of Emperor Charles IV at St. Denis (Plate 7). Here, the joints in the pavement create the impression that they are the product of a curved perspective construction. One possible explanation for these curves is that Fouquet used a convex mirror. Nevertheless, he was well versed in central perspective theory through his trip to Italy, and curved lines like these have nothing in common with Albertian perspective, the latter having taken it as axiomatic that vertical lines and lines running parallel to the picture plane remain parallel.

The reason for Fouquet's curved environments may be that he consciously sought to break through existing laws of perspective, for in several respects they did not, in fact, reflect visual experience.[5] When we stand in front of the facade of a wide building and let our eyes travel from left to right, the building seems to become smaller as our eyes move away from center. But, according to Alberti, the building must be drawn in such a way that the roofline runs parallel to the groundline. Naturally, his thesis has merits, for in reality they *do* run parallel. In fact, Alberti here makes a concession to reality and to the aesthetic appearance of a painting, at the expense of subjective visual experience.

But when a plane that runs parallel to the picture is to be represented in central perspective, as for example in the just-mentioned facade, the visual "error" at the ends will actually be corrected if the facade is seen from a predetermined distance and with only one eye. The areas left and right of center-picture will then occupy a narrower visual angle.[6] This state of affairs changes, however, when the distance between the eye and the picture plane is short and when no two-dimensional objects, but only three-dimensional ones, are shown.

## Leonardo da Vinci

After the discovery of anamorphosis had been attributed to Leonardo da Vinci, the Leonardo scholar Carlo Pedretti began to look for passages in the notes Leonardo made for his envisioned treatise on painting that could be connected with the discovery. Various notes make it clear that Leonardo had investigated the contradictions in central perspective mentioned above.[7]

Leonardo distinguished between natural perspective—based on ancient optics—and artificial perspective, Alberti's construction, which is used in art.

In natural perspective, we seek to discover rules that reflect our own observation. One important rule of this sort states that our angle of vision decreases as the distance between us and an object increases. The distances between lines that in Alberti's artificial perspective run parallel to the picture plane become ever smaller. In reality, of course, the inverse effect is being produced: As one sees the painted objects growing smaller in size, because the visual angle from which they are seen decreases, the painter is creating the impression that the distance between us and them is increasing.

According to Leonardo, it is possible to combine natural and artificial perspective in one picture. "By natural perspective," writes Leonardo, "I mean that the plane on which this [artificial] perspective is represented is a flat surface, and this plane, although it is parallel both in length and height, is forced to diminish in its remoter [from our point of view] parts more than in its nearer ones."

Then Leonardo gives a rather subtle example of artificial perspective: "Let this plane be 'd–e,' on which are seen three equal circles which are beyond this plane 'd–e,' that is the circles 'a, b, c.' Now you see that the eye, 'A,' sees on the vertical plane the sections of the images, largest of those that are farthest and smallest of the nearest"[8] (Fig. 10).

In this way, he proved that artificial perspective is somewhat different from natural perspective. For in this case the size of the pictured objects at the sides seems greater, though they are farther away. An "exaggerated" artificial perspective of this construction, as we have seen, would require a single viewer who looks from a fixed point through a hole; for all other viewers, the representation would be merely chaotic.[9]

At another point, Leonardo varies his interpretation, however. He gives a new example and calls it a combination of natural and artificial perspective (Fig. 11). "Let us say then that the square 'a–b–c–d' . . . is 25

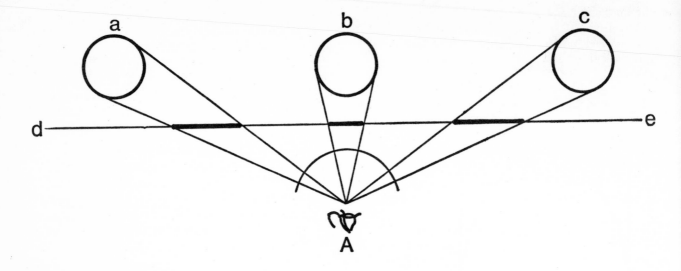

*Fig. 10* After Leonardo da Vinci. Ms. A, fol. 38 recto. 1492. Institut de France, Paris

In this sketch Leonardo tries to show that objects (in this case circles) that are farther from the observation point appear larger than those that are nearer.

*Fig. 11* Leonardo da Vinci. Codex Arundel, fol. 62 recto. c. 1480. British Museum, London

When the distorted forms on the left are observed from the viewpoint that has been established through normal perspective at the right, one should be able to see precisely the same forms. Here we are dealing with a theoretical proposition rather than a controllable fact.

*Fig. 12* Leonardo da Vinci. Ms. A, fol. 42 verso. 1492. Institut de France, Paris

If one casts and traces the shadow of an object (in this case a sphere) on a wall and then observes this outline from the point at which the light source stood, the drawing seems correct and tangible. Here Leonardo gives the first practical guide to the construction of a perspective anamorphosis.

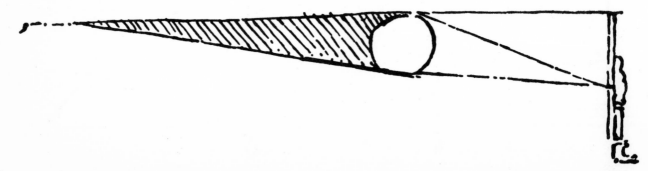

foreshortened being seen by the eye situated in the center of the side which is in front. But a mixture of artificial and natural perspective will be seen in this tetragon called *el main* [?], that is to say 'e–f–g–h' which must appear to the eye of the spectator to be equal to 'a-b-c-d' so long as the eye remains in its first position between 'c' and 'd.' And this will be seen to

have a good effect, because the natural perspective of the plane will conceal the defects which would [otherwise] seem monstrous."[10]

Here, Leonardo cleared the path for the anamorphic construction, which developed in natural fashion as a peripheral manifestation of artificial perspective. He gives one other practical piece of

*Fig. 13*  Albrecht Dürer. *Underweysung der Messung . . .* (Nuremberg, 1525), illus. 16

When inscriptions have to be placed on high walls, Dürer advises that the letters be made larger as they go upward. He assumes that the angle of vision remains constant (cf. Fig. 10).

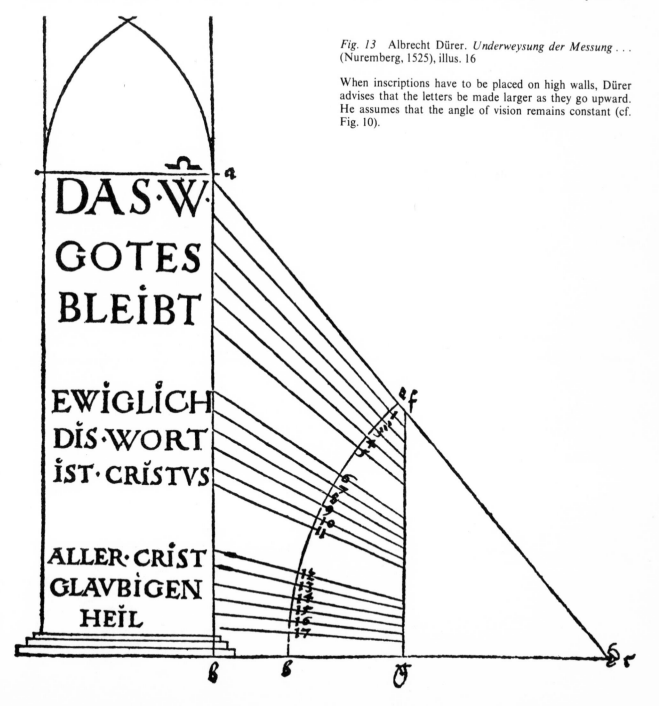

guidance. "If you want to represent a figure on a wall, the wall being foreshortened, while the figure is to appear in its proper form, and as standing free from the wall, you must proceed thus: Have a thin plate of iron and make a small hole in the center; this hole must be round. Set a light close to it in such a position that it shines through the central hole, then place any object or figure you please so close to the wall that it touches it and draw the outline of the shadow on the wall; then fill in the shade and add the lights; place the person who is to see it so that he looks through the same hole where at first the light was; and you will never be able to persuade yourself that the image is not detached from the wall."[11]

Beyond this experimental method for creating anamorphic projections, this description alludes to a fascinating special effect of the anamorphosis: The anamorphic representation rises from the background and finds its own separate existence in front of it.

A necessity for all these phenomena is a viewpoint close to the picture surface. For "normal" pictures, Leonardo therefore recommended a distance between image and eye at least three times as great as the height of the image. This makes it possible for more than one viewer to look at the picture at the same time. Also, then, when one takes a different position from the ideal one, the picture offers a satisfactory aspect.[12]

Notes

1  Pomponio Gaurico, *De Sculptura*, ed. A. Chastel and R. Klein (Paris, 1969), pp. 182–83.
2  For a discussion of the exact nature of Brunelleschi's paintings, see S. Y. Edgerton, Jr., "Brunelleschi's First Perspective Picture," *Arte Lombarda* 38/39 (1973): 172–95, and Bibliography.
3  Leonbattista Alberti, *On Painting and on Sculpture*, ed. C. Grayson (London, 1972).
4  M. A. Lavin, "Piero della Francesca: The Flagellation," in *Art in Context* (New York, 1972), pp. 38–45.
5  J. White, *The Birth and Rebirth of Pictorial Space* (London, 1957), pp. 226–27.
6  See R. Klein, *La Forme et l'intelligible* (Paris, 1970), pp. 289–93.
7  C. Pedretti, *Studio Vinciani* (Geneva, 1957).
8  Leonardo da Vinci, Ms. E, fol. 16b. Paris, Institut de France. See *The Notebooks of Leonardo da Vinci*, ed. J. P. Richter (New York, 1970), vol. 1, p. 63.
9  *Ibid.*, fol. 16a. See Richter, *op cit.*, vol. 1, pp. 63–64.
10  Leonardo da Vinci, Codex Arundel, fol. 62a. London, British Museum. See Richter, *op. cit.*, vol. 1, p. 65.
11  Leonardo da Vinci, Ms. A, fol. 42b. Paris, Institute de France. See Richter, *op cit.*, vol. 1, p. 262.
12  *Ibid.*, fol. 38a. See Richter, *op cit.*, vol. 1, p. 55.

*Captions to the following plates are on pages 45–46*

5

6

7

8

9

10

11

12

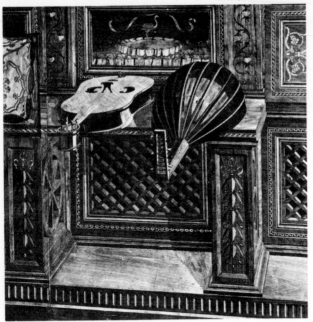

13

14

15

16

17 ▷

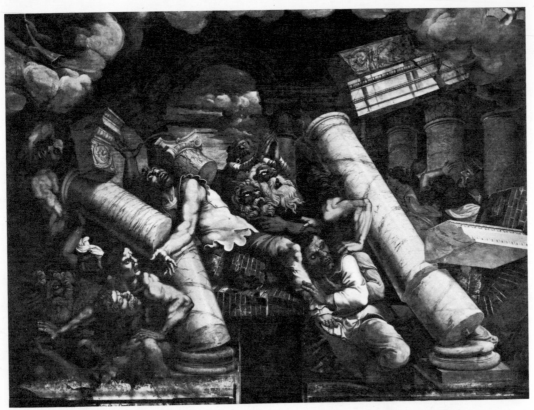

20

21

23

24

25

27

28

29

30

31

32

33

34

35

5 Piero della Francesca. *The Flagellation of Christ*. c. 1460. Tempera on panel, 22¾ x 32⅛″ (58.4 x 81.5 cm). Palazzo Ducale, Urbino

Mathematical precision helped create a bright and lucid space. The scale of the figures and the buildings was determined by perspective construction (cf. Fig. 9).

6 Conrad Witz. *Madonna and Saints in a Church*. 1442–43. Oil on panel, 25 x 17⅝″ (63.5 x 44.3 cm). Museo di Capodimonte, Naples

From the curves in the architecture we can assume that the artist used a convex mirror to enlarge his angle of vision.

7 Jean Fouquet. *The Arrival of Emperor Charles IV at St. Denis*, from *Grandes Chroniques des rois de France*. 1458. Bibliothèque Nationale, Paris (Ms. fr. 6465, fol. 444)

In this miniature the curving lines of the pavement are very expressive. If one glances from left to right, one can follow the movement of the imperial group.

8 Masaccio. *The Trinity*. c. 1427–28. Fresco. S. Maria Novella, Florence

Because Masaccio fixes his perspective according to the standpoint of the viewer, he creates the impression that the painted space in his fresco is a continuation of the actual space in which the viewer stands.

9 Paolo Uccello. *Equestrian Portrait of Sir John Hawkwood*. 1436. Fresco. Cathedral, Florence

A fresco with illusionistic perspective here successfully substituted for a bronze equestrian statue.

10 Donatello. *The Miracle of the Mule*. c. 1447. Bronze altar relief. S. Antonio, Padua

11 Andrea Mantegna. *Saint James Led to His Execution*. After 1453. Fresco. Church of the Eremitani, Padua (destroyed 1944)

Influenced by the work of Donatello, Mantegna accentuated the illusion of depth by an impressive piece of vaulted architecture. The fresco is painted in such a way that we seem to be looking upward at an actual event.

12 Andrea Mantegna. Ceiling fresco in the Camera degli Sposi. 1473. Palazzo Ducale, Mantua

This perspective masterpiece embodies the highest development of Mantegna's illusionism. The ceiling painting was constructed according to the upward gaze of the viewer.

13–17 Baccio Pontelli. Intarsia paneling in the study of Federigo da Montefeltro. 1476. Palazzo Ducale, Urbino (details)

13 Small console table with musical instruments

14 The same detail as in Plate 13, but this time seen from an incorrect viewpoint

15 Still lifes on console table and in cabinets

16 The same detail as in Plate 15, seen from an incorrect viewpoint

17 Cabinets with books; portrait of Federigo da Montefeltro in a toga

18 Detail of ceiling fresco in Plate 19

If one compares the painting with the actual architecture below, its distortion becomes evident.

19 Andrea Pozzo. *Entrance of Saint Ignatius into Paradise*. 1691–94. Fresco. S. Ignazio, Rome

The ceiling of the nave of this large church is heightened by a colossal painting that seems to extend the architecture dizzingly upward. The fresco is filled with allegorical figures. A marble slab in the floor indicates the place where one must stand in order to experience the illusion best. This fresco comes at the end of the long development of *quadratura* painting (illusionistic painting of architectural perspectives), and is one of the most powerful examples of its kind.

20 Giulio Romano (project) and Rinaldo Mantovano. *Fall of the Giants*. 1532–34. Fresco. Sala dei Giganti, Palazzo del Te, Mantua

The colossal figures ignore the real architecture, which seems literally to be collapsing.

21 Andrea Pozzo. False dome. 1684–85. Oil on canvas. S. Ignazio, Rome

Since the monks at a nearby monastery were afraid that a dome on this Jesuit church would darken their library, it was decided to have a painted rather than a real one. Pozzo won the competition for the commission. The illusion is so persuasive that one cannot believe one is looking at a flat surface. Here, too, a marble slab indicates the place to stand.

22, 23 Andrea Pozzo. Corridor to the apartments of Saint Ignatius. Begun 1682. Fresco. Casa Professa, II Gesù, Rome

When one enters the corridor (Plate 22), the painting on the wall looks chaotic. But when one reaches the center of the passage (Plate 23), the bizarre forms arrange themselves into an archway that entirely ignores the actual barrel vault and flat walls. The transverse wall at the end of the corridor is punctuated by a false altar 45 before which an angel playing a musical instrument seems to sit. The effect of the distortion is particularly convincing in the beamed ceiling. Seen from the proper viewpoint, the barrel vault seems to be an impossibility. When one moves on, nothing remains of the elaborate arches and figures but abstract configurations (see Plates 63–66).

24, 25    Details of Plates 22, 23
Seen from the proper viewpoint it looks as though the putti are standing *in front of* the painting. This results from the anamorphic distortion of these figures, in which the rest of the painting itself does not partake.

26, 27    Donato Bramante. False choir in stucco. 1483–86. S. Maria presso S. Satiro, Milan
Since the street behind the church made it impossible to build a choir, Bramante was forced—if he wanted to retain harmonious proportions—to find a special solution. An unsuspecting visitor to the church does not notice until he stands very close to it that the whole choir is nothing but a relief four feet deep. Yet a glance into the righthand transept serves to make one realize the only apparent similarity of the actual space and the fictive choir (Plate 26).

28    Gianlorenzo Bernini. St. Peter's Square. 1656–67. The Vatican
The semicircular colonnades that surround the square are connected to the facade of St. Peter's by straight rows of columns. The colonnades veer away from each other slightly in the direction of the church (cf. also Plate 29). As a result, St. Peter's seems to dominate the square even more noticeably.

29    Michelangelo. The Campidoglio. Begun 1538. Rome
The two palaces left and right diverge slightly toward the rear. Through this extended perspective, the Palazzo Senatorio on the far side of the piazza appears larger than it really is (cf. Fig. 21).

30, 31    Tullio Lombardo. Perspective reliefs: *Scenes from the Life of Saint Mark*. Left, *The Healing of Anianus*; right, *The Baptism of Anianus*. c. 1490. Scuola di S. Marco, Venice
If one walks over the bridge to SS. Giovanni e Paolo and looks to the left, the facade reliefs of the Scuola di S. Marco give the impression of real architecture (Plate 30). The effect of Donatello's relief (Plate 10) is here carried out on a lifesize scale.

32, 34, 35    Gianlorenzo Bernini. Scala Regia (Royal Staircase). 1663–66. The Vatican
The majestic colonnades to the left and right of the staircase conceal the obliqueness of the original walls. The uniform reduction in width from the bottom—15′9″ (4.8 m)—to the top—11′2″ (3.4 m)—and the inconsistent lighting create a theatrical effect. The whole appears even grander than it really is.

33    Antonio da Sangallo the Younger. Vestibule in the Palazzo Farnese, Rome. 1541–46
To bring the monumental vestibule of the Palazzo Farnese, with its two side aisles, into harmony with the arches of the arcade around the inner courtyard, the builder filled the lunettes over the entrances to the side aisles with fan-shaped reliefs. When one looks at this relief from a particular angle, it creates the perspective illusion of depth.

# 3. Illusionism

Perspective not only is a way of organizing a picture internally; it also offers a means of coordinating it with the position of the viewer.

When Alberti recommended his "chessboard" pavement as a framework for the construction of his perspective, he added that the squares must bear a relation to the human scale. In his terms, "human scale" implies the size of the figures in the picture. The length of the divisions at the base of the picture was established by dividing the height of the images in the foreground by three. The horizon was placed at the eye-level of these figures. Thus Alberti adjusted his perspective to the particular event that the painting, the "historia," was to relate and the figures to enact.[1]

But even before Alberti formulated these rules, painters had experimented with other ways of using the new device.

In the famous *Trinity* fresco in Florence's S. Maria Novella, which must have been painted in 1427–28, the vanishing point and the horizon line do not reflect the eye-level of the figures but are placed at the eye-level of the viewer (Plate 8). The impression made is that the painted architecture is an extension of the real world; the space in which the observer stands and that of the painted image are a continuum.

The particular type of illusionistic effect found in the *Trinity* fresco was not widely adopted in Florence. One of the few other examples is the equestrian portrait of the English condottiere Sir John Hawkwood, painted for Florence cathedral by Paolo Uccello (Plate 9). The choice of the illusionistic technique had an unusual point here. John Hawkwood had stipulated in his will that a bronze equestrian statue of himself be erected in the church in his memory. This idea was discarded after his death; his employers—the city council—found that a substitute picture would meet the wishes of the deceased well enough. By choosing a very low viewpoint for the lower part of the pedestal, Uccello nearly convinces us that we are actually looking at the bronze statue Hawkwood had ordered. And, in keeping with Hawkwood's dignity, horse and rider are shown in a squarely frontal position.

The illusionistic method of representation enjoyed a much greater popularity in northern Italy. Beginning in 1447, the Florentine sculptor Donatello worked in Padua on the high altar for S. Antonio, the church dedicated to the city's patron saint. He made a number of bronze reliefs for this, showing scenes from the life of the saint. The perspective and the low horizon are most powerfully effective in the relief of *The Miracle of the Mule* (Plate 10). The story, for unbelievers a most persuasive demonstration of the power of the eucharist, takes place in an impressive vaulted space; the vanishing point lies below the lower border of the relief.

Andrea Mantegna very quickly comprehended the possibilities that this kind of representation offered. A few years after Donatello's Paduan reliefs were completed, Mantegna painted a series of frescoes in the Church of the Eremitani in Padua that depicted the passion of St. James. In one of the finest of these (Plate 11), we see James led to his execution. The perspective here is directed upward at such an extreme angle that the ground is below our view.

The ultimate in this highly subjective form of perspective directed exclusively at the viewer is found in Mantegna's Camera degli Sposi in the Palazzo Ducale in Mantua (Plate 12). The frescoes on the walls work with the actual space of the room to create a visual unity, and in the center of the ceiling is an apparent opening. Past the parapet, beyond the court ladies who peep down at us, giggling, and the putti tumbling energetically about, we look up into blue sky.

To depict the unbounded extension of circumscribed space was also a favorite pastime of the fifteenth-century craftsmen who made inlaid wood mosaics, or intarsie, to decorate furniture and rooms. They could achieve such striking illusionistic effects with their two-dimensional pieces of veneer in different shadings that one scarcely can discern what is reality and what appearance.

In the middle of the sixteenth century, the painter and artists' biographer Giorgio Vasari wrote that

Brunelleschi had earlier recommended his perspective technique to the intarsia artists.[2]

Until Brunelleschi's time, they had limited themselves to fashioning surfaces in a flat, decorative way out of different kinds of wood. Their work—full of sharp edges and contours—was very easily adapted to the rendering of complicated geometric forms. About the middle of the fifteenth century, they were described in the city archives of Florence simply as "maestri di prospettiva" (masters of perspective).

One of the cleverest uses to which this technique was turned is found in the ducal palace of Urbino.

Here, in the little study of Duke Federigo da Montefeltro, Baccio Pontelli created an environment in wood. The inlay depicts, among other things, a half-open cupboard, an architectural perspective with a view of distant countryside, carelessly scattered musical instruments, open books, and small statuettes wearing fluttering robes (Plates 13–17).

The shadows correspond exactly to the fall of light through open doors on the windowed walls. When the visitor stands in mid-room, the walls dissolve into an exalted, humanistic illusion.

Notes

1   Leonbattista Alberti, *On Painting and on Sculpture*, ed. C. Grayson (London, 1972).

2   Antonio Manetti worked in intarsia.

# 4. Curved and Discontinuous Picture Planes

When the viewpoint of the observer—that is, his position in actual space—is the painter's point of departure in constructing his framework of perspective, the surface of his picture loses its value as an active element in the composition. In this case, it is important only that the observer perceive the painted world as a part of the space in which he stands. The painted surface—in actual fact, the bearer of this intelligence—must nevertheless recede.

Customarily, fresco painters had to master the technique not only of painting flat walls but also of decorating vaults. The problems posed by the curves and corners could be "solved" by the new system when one projected the perspective-plan on the chosen surface.

Paolo Uccello, that perennial experimenter, seems to have solved this problem very early. Sadly, we are dependent on the written record here also for our knowledge of this work. In his *Lives of the Most Eminent Painters, Sculptors, and Architects*, published in Florence in 1550 and 1568, Vasari describes a work of Uccello's that must have been executed about the middle of the fifteenth century, an *Annunciation* in the church of S. Maria Maggiore in Florence. Its perspective had indeed to be described as sensational. In this painting, Vasari writes, Uccello demonstrated "how a small and restricted space on a flat surface may be extended so that it appears distant and large." According to Vasari, Uccello was not satisfied, but "wanted to show how to solve even greater problems; and this he did in some columns foreshortened in perspective which curve around and break the salient angle of the vaulting where the four Evangelists are."[1]

Uccello was thus probably the first to create a wall painting that flowed convincingly over onto the ceiling above; in doing this, the picture must have seemed, in Vasari's description, to "break the salient angle of the vaulting." To do this, he chose a subject that would give the illusion most effective play, and the imaginary architecture of the columns effortlessly bypassed the real architecture of the church.

Vasari does not disclose whether the four Evangelists and the vaulting were placed in the same foreshortening. In Leonardo's writings, too, we find an illustrated description of a process by which one can create figures that "break through" from one type of surface to another.

In the notes for his projected treatise on painting, Leonardo sets himself the problem of how to make a rendering of a figure that should appear 24 braccias high (about 47 feet, or 14.40 meters) on a wall that is 12 braccias high (about 23 feet 6 inches, or 7.20 meters). The lower half of the figure causes no difficulty: It is simply drawn on a line he designates as "m–r." The curvature of the vault "m–n," however, poses a problem. In order to project the figure on the vault—a curved surface—one must first draw it in profile and full extension. Then, all the important points of the figure are connected with the viewpoint of the observer, "f." The places where these connecting lines cut the vaulting "m–n" create a framework for the foreshortened representation of the rest of the figure (Fig. 14). When a figure of this sort is looked at through a frame or a peephole, it produces a particularly convincing effect.[2]

Leonardo mentions this method of creating an illusion along with a description of anamorphoses. Both methods involve a perspective that, while breaking through, is nevertheless fixed to a tangible painted surface, with all the distortion that comes with it. In the anamorphic construction, the extensive spatial reality of natural perspective is closely confined; in illusionistic vault painting, the actual picture surface is also ignored in order to create the stage for a painterly illusion. Both, however, are based on one postulate: that their construction must be synchronized with the observer's eye. In order to enjoy the illusion, one must look through a peephole or take a specific position that fixes one's view of the picture. These techniques offer the key to the restriction or expansion of real space. It goes without saying that it is more exciting to make spaces seem larger than they are, and thus many frescoes were painted in the sixteenth century, in palaces and churches, that seem to extend the actual

*Fig. 14* Leonardo da Vinci. Ms. A, fol. 38 verso. 1492. Institut de France, Paris

On a wall that turns into an arch a figure can be projected that seems twice the height of the painted area.

architecture into infinity, without relation to the actual size of the room or the shape of the walls and ceilings.

The culmination of this development lies in the work of Andrea Pozzo, a Jesuit, who also was an architect, painter, and writer of treatises. In his oeuvre a high point was reached in this kind of illusionism, which is called *quadratura* painting.[3]

A variety of examples of Pozzo's genius are to be found in the church of S. Ignazio in Rome. In his treatise on perspective—*Perspectivae Pictorum atque Architectorum*, which first appeared in 1693 in Rome—he deals extensively with the methods by which he decorated the vault of the nave of this church and painted an illusionistic composition in the dome over the transept.[4]

S. Ignazio, one of the most important of the Jesuit churches, was built between 1626 and 1650. In its design, this church is strongly reminiscent of the church of Il Gesù and, as there, a dome was originally to have been built over the crossing; however, when the church was opened to the public in 1650, it still had no dome. The design for a huge one alarmed the neighboring Dominicans, who feared that it would rob their library of much light. A competition for a new solution was announced, and in 1684 all were at last agreed: the crossing would be capped not by a real but by a painted dome. Pozzo, who already had had some experience with such work, received the commission. In 1685 he finished the project, and even today one can imagine the astonishment of the public at the ceremonial unveiling.

When one enters the church and takes the correct position—marked by a marble slab in the floor beneath the "dome"—it is almost impossible to realize that one is looking at a flat canvas (Plate 21). The optical illusion is very strong, the "architecture" less so. In his book, Pozzo recounts that several architects commented that the columns in the "dome" rest on consoles, and that such construction would not be solid enough in a real building. Pozzo replied ironically: "A certain painter with whom I am very intimate has solemnly sworn to me that he will bear all damages and charges if the bearing stones ever break and the poor columns come tumbling down."[5]

Pozzo worked for three years on his next project, a huge illusionistic ceiling painting in the nave of S. Ignazio: *Entrance of Saint Ignatius into Paradise* (Plates 18, 19). In the center, the saint is carried up to heaven, while the four continents, converted to the faith, attest from the earth to his glory. Here, too, a marble slab in the floor indicates the place from which the illusion is complete.[6] Even when one gazes up intently, one finds it difficult to determine the border between the real and the painted architecture. Happily, in his book Pozzo gives detailed instructions on how he created such paintings. He began by drawing the architecture that he wished to paint as though it were a real extension of the church (Fig. 15). Then he turned it into a "horizontal perspective"; that is, he projected the whole picture on a horizontal surface, following the rules of perspective according to which the viewpoint is determined by the distance of the viewer from an imaginary horizontal surface (Fig. 16). This surface Pozzo located in the nave, at the point where the vertical wall curved into the barrel vault. He made a model of this step—the projection on a flat surface—which is now in the Galleria Nazionale in Rome.

The real problem—and also the close relationship with anamorphosis—was created when this flat projection had to be transferred to the curved vault of the church[7] (Fig. 17). Pozzo's solution was to stretch a network ("N") in place of the imaginary horizontal projection. The simplest method now would have been to place a light source at viewpoint "o" and to trace the shadows that it cast on the vault. This method was, however, not easily carried out, for the shadows were too fuzzy in those areas where the distance between the vault and the network—seen from the chosen viewpoint—became too large. Here Pozzo turned to projection. He stretched string up from viewpoint "o" and used it instead of a beam of light to transfer the lines of the network to the vault. The distorted rectangles that were then projected on the vault were filled in in the same relationship to the network in which the sketch was divided.

Because of the great distance between the viewer's eye and the vault, it is impossible, from the correct viewing position, to detect the actual shape of the ceiling. Only the figures remind us that we are looking at a painting. When one moves away from the ideal standpoint, the spatial illusion decreases little by little, but a distorted impression nevertheless remains. Compared to the real architecture, this distortion is unmistakable (Plate 18).

The way Pozzo went about his task is not essentially different from the way anamorphoses were constructed in his day. When the picture surface is imaginary—as is the *quadratura*, the grid—then it makes no difference what position or what form the actual painted surface takes.

The connection with anamorphosis is clearer in another example of Pozzo's work: the decoration on the walls of a corridor that in the Casa Professa near the Gesù led to the apartments of St. Ignatius (begun 1682).[8]

This very shallow space (Plates 22, 23) offers a shorter viewing distance, and we have already seen that the edge-distortion becomes much greater in such cases. The perspective is constructed from a viewpoint at the middle of the passage. When the observer stands there, it seems as if there were no vaulting at all. Heavy arches resting on consoles fill the ceiling. But if one walks to the end of the corridor, the distortions become grotesque (see Plates 63–66).

The unusually plastic quality of this anamorphic projection is particularly strong in the areas where scenes from the life of St. Ignatius are painted on the walls. These *quadri riportati*, or inset pictures, stand apart from the illusionistic system and disclose themselves as flat surfaces. They are in marked contrast to the putti with flowers that seem to float free of the surface and arouse the impression that they are standing in front of the paintings; if one looks at them directly from the front, one sees that this impression is caused by their horizontal anamorphic distortion.

In this illusionary art, the unintelligibility that is the most distinctive feature of anamorphosis is not the main objective. Yet the same method is used: The surface to be painted does not coincide with the imaginary picture surface. The main thing here is the visual impression that the representation is detached from its background.

36  Andrea Palladio (?), Vincenzo Scamozzi. Perspective stage setting. c. 1581–85. Teatro Olimpico, Vicenza

The upward slant of the stage and the diminition of the proportions in the background create—within a confined space—the impression of a long street.

37–41  Francesco Borromini. Colonnade in the Palazzo Spada, Rome. c. 1635

Here Borromini created a colonnade for his patron that at first glance seems much deeper than it really is, 28'2" (8.58 m). This marginal architectural activity borders on stage illusion.

42, 43  Guarino Guarini. Dome of the Cappella della S. Sindone, Turin. 1668–94

Through the regular reduction in size of intersecting geometrical elements of the same shape, the impression is created within that the dome is a very tall light-shaft, although, viewed from outside, it is seen to be of merely modest height (Plate 42).

44  Anonymous south Netherlandish. Perspective anamorphosis: *The Witches of Endor; Saul Falls on His Sword*. Second half of the sixteenth century. Oil on panel. Private collection, Germany

At left the witches predict Saul's fate; at right the apparition of its fulfillment hovers in ghostly distortion against the windswept landscape.

45  Niccolò dell'Abate (?). Perspective anamorphosis: *Landscape with Pastoral Scenes and Saint Jerome*. Above, *The Baptism of Christ;* below, *The Head of John the Baptist on a Platter*. Last quarter of the sixteenth century. Oil on panel, 16⅞ x 35⅜" (43 x 90 cm). Collection Cacetta, Rome

46  Emmanuel Maignan. *Perspectiva horaria....* (Rome, 1648), p. 438—an engraving that explains how Maignan executed his fresco *Saint Francis of Paola* (see Plates 47–50)

All points on the original drawing "a-b-e-f," which is attached to the wall with hinges, are, with the help of threads, projected from viewpoint "N" on the wall with a movable plumb on a string F-H.

47–50  Emmanuel Maignan. Anamorphic fresco: *Saint Francis of Paola*. 1642. Monastery of SS. Trinità dei Monti, Rome

The sole surviving large-scale perspective anamorphosis is in the monastery of the Minims in Rome. From one end of the corridor, everything seems in proper proportion (Plate 48), but the nearer one approaches, the more incomprehensible the forms become (Plate 47). Between the folds of Saint Francis's cowl there appears a view of the Straits of Messina, the scene of one of his miracles (Plate 50).

51  Anonymous French. *Physics Hall*. c. 1700. Engraving (unfinished)

In the foreground various anamorphoses are pictured. They belong to the realm of the natural sciences.

52  Anonymous French. *The Académie des Sciences et des Beaux-Arts*. c. 1700. Oil on canvas, 18⅞ x 37⅜" (48 x 95 cm). Collection Monnier, Paris

This canvas portrays the art of painting as a science among sciences. Anamorphosis and perspective, which both require a "scientific" approach, occupy a prominent position in the foreground.

53  Photograph of one of the reflecting cylinders in the collection of mirrors and reflectors at the Musée du Conservatoire National des Arts et Métiers, Paris

54  Cone anamorphosis: *Two Seashells* (see caption to Plates 106, 107)

55  Henry Kettle. Cone anamorphosis: *Venus and Adonis*. c. 1770. Oil on panel, 27⅛ x 26¾" (69 x 68 cm). Private collection, Milan

Kettle took this composition from an engraving (1638) that Michel Dorigny made after a painting by Simon Vouet, which is in Leningrad. The engraving differs in some details (trees, dogs) from the painting. The violent deformation of Vouet's classicist composition makes this anamorphosis particularly amusing.

56  Henry Kettle. Cone anamorphosis: *A Wild Boar Defends Its Young Against a Dog*. c. 1770. Oil on panel, 26¾ x 27⅛" (68 x 69 cm). Private collection, Milan

A cylinder anamorphosis from Leiden (Plate 155) is signed "Hen : Kettle pixt." When one looks in the cylinder, one discovers the same composition that appears here in the cone. The cone must be viewed directly from above. The style also seems almost the same in the two versions. Both paintings can be ascribed with certainty to Henry Kettle. And consequently, a great many other anamorphoses can be credited to him. In the same collection in Milan and in a private collection in Amsterdam are various paintings for the reflecting cone which come from the same hand and follow the same format as the hunt scene (Plates 55, 57–59).

57  Henry Kettle. Cone anamorphosis: *An Owl Defends Her Young*. c. 1770. Oil on panel, 27⅛ x 26¾" (69 x 68 cm). Private collection, Milan

The pastoral and hunt scenes which Kettle fashioned probably had their genesis in the flat animal paintings of the circle of Pieter de Vos and Jan Fyt.

58  Henry Kettle. Cone anamorphosis: *A Woman, Seated on a Donkey, Offers Food to a Dog*. c. 1770. Oil on panel, 27⅛ x 26¾" (69 x 68 cm). Private collection, Milan

37

38

39

40

41

42

43

44

45

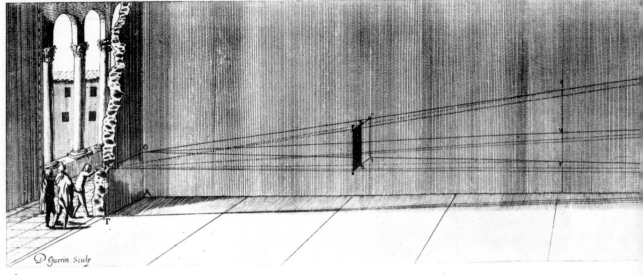

46

47

48

49

50

51
52                                                                                          53 ▷

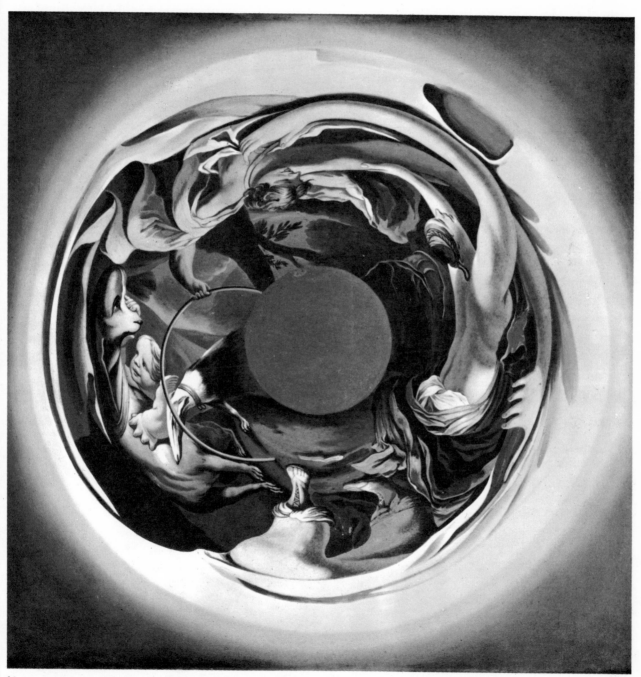

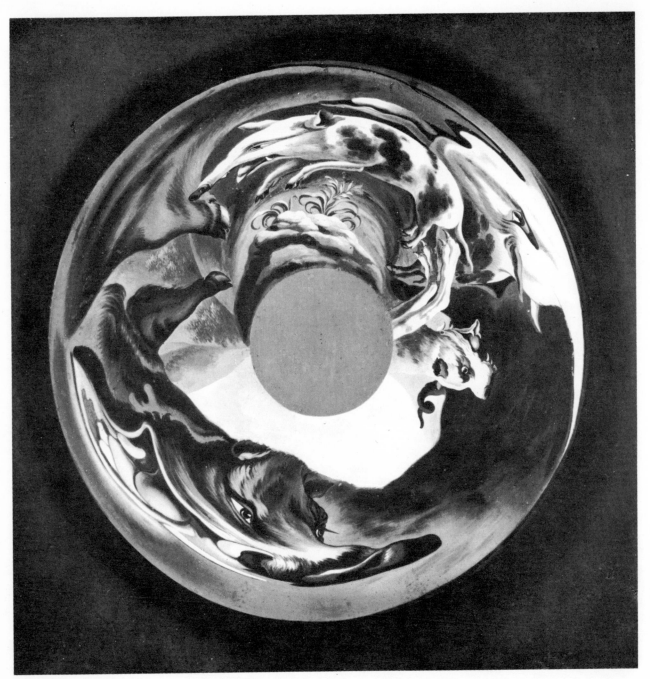

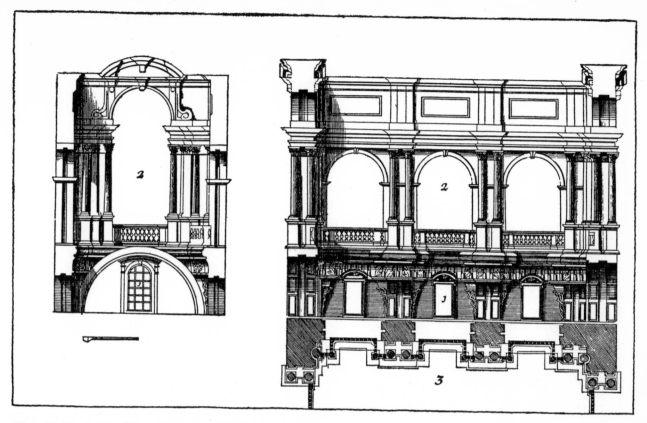

*Figs. 15–17* Andrea Pozzo. *Perspectivae Pictorum atque Architectorum . . .* (Augsburg, 1708), illus. 96, 99, 100

*Fig. 15 (above)* In his book Pozzo describes the method he used to execute the ceiling fresco in the nave of S. Ignazio (see Plates 18, 19). As a first step he designed an architectural background for the figures that would look like a continuation of the real building. Here, only the windows (*1*) would be genuine.

*Fig. 16 (below)* The whole was then projected—with the desired ornamentation and lighting—onto a flat surface, as if one were looking up at the architecture from below.

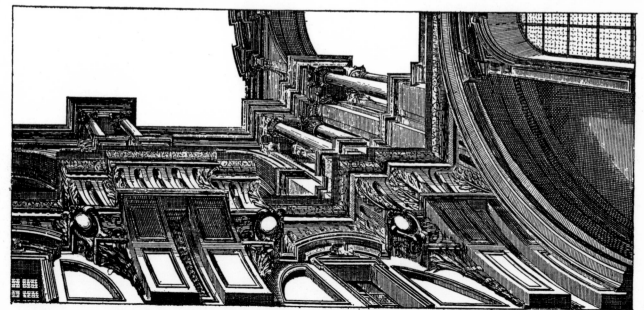

Notes

1  Giorgio Vasari, *The Lives of the Artists*, trans. George Bull (Harmondsworth–Baltimore, 1965), p. 97.

2  Leonardo da Vinci, Ms. A, fol. 38b. Paris, Institut de France. See *The Notebooks of Leonardo da Vinci*, ed. J. P. Richter (New York, 1970), vol. 1, p. 263.

3  "Prospettici e Quadraturisti," in *Enciclopedia niversale dell'Arte*.

4  B. Kerber, *Andrea Pozzo* (Berlin–New York, 1971), pp. 54–74.

5  Andrea Pozzo, *Perspectivae Pictorum atque Architectorum....* (Augsburg, 1708).

6  B. Kerber, *op. cit.*, pp. 94–98.

7  M. H. Pirenne, *Optics, Painting, and Photography* (New York, 1970), pp. 79–94.

8  B. Kerber, *op. cit.*, pp. 50–54.

*Fig. 17*  The nave of the church was then spanned with a network of strings so that a flat surface was projected from a chosen viewpoint onto the curved surface of the vaulting. The design was divided into corresponding squares and could then be transferred to the ceiling.

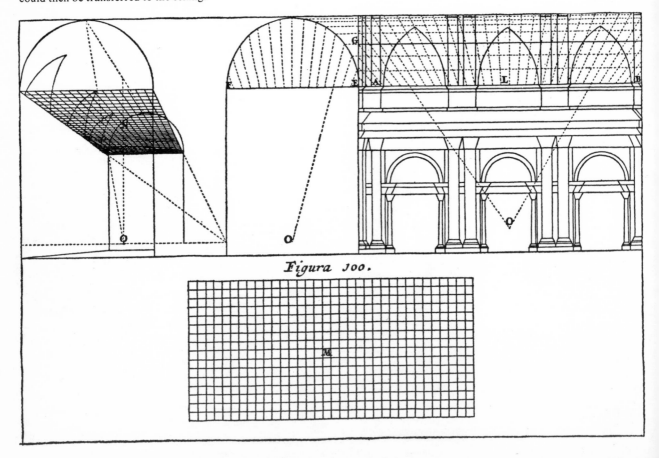

# 5. Architecture and Theater

After Masaccio's *Trinity*, painters of lifesize frescoes found themselves faced with a difficulty. The colored surfaces of their paintings contrasted too strongly with their stone surroundings. Bordered by architecture, as color and as surface they yet bore no real relationship to their settings. Donatello's bronze reliefs—even his marble reliefs—were too painterly for another reason. In the spaces they simulated, another scale applied, the scale of panel painting.

The thirty-three-year-old Donato Bramante was active in 1477 as a painter of large-scale decorative frescoes. Since he worked in northern Italy and later became the most famous architect of the High Renaissance, one may assume that he was acquainted with Mantegna's illusionistic work.[1] Moreover, his paintings and those attributed to him have a strongly illusionistic character. His name is also linked to Duke Federigo da Montefeltro's study in Urbino and its refined illusionistic decoration.[2]

When, in 1483, he began work on his first large architectural commission, the reconstruction of S. Maria presso S. Satiro in Milan, he had behind him an exemplary apprenticeship as a painter of perspective .

On the spot where the church was to be rebuilt there stood a small Carolingian chapel dedicated to St. Satyrus. In 1479, a simple one-aisled church had been added to this chapel so that a picture of the Virgin could be worshiped there. While work was still in progress, it was decided to build a much larger church.

In the plan Bramante proposed in 1483, the existing building became merely the transept of the new one (Fig. 18). Attached to it at right angles, a new nave

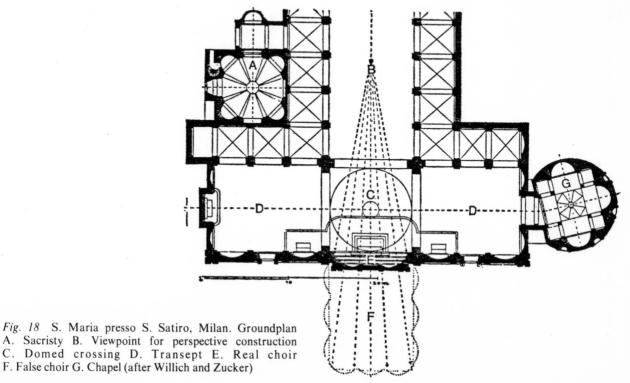

*Fig. 18* S. Maria presso S. Satiro, Milan. Groundplan A. Sacristy B. Viewpoint for perspective construction C. Domed crossing D. Transept E. Real choir F. False choir G. Chapel (after Willich and Zucker)

with side aisles was built. Nave and transept were roofed with a massive coffered barrel vault, and a dome covered the crossing.

Normally, the nave would have extended past the transept into a choir, but a street on the east side of the building made it seem that the otherwise handsomely proportioned interior space must remain incomplete.

Today, one looks down the nave to a choir that cannot be distinguished in its proportions or detailing from the rest of the building. Moving closer, however, one discovers that this first impression was false. The entire choir, with its vault and arcading, shrinks to a stucco relief about two yards deep (Plates 26, 27).

With one ingenious stroke, Bramante escaped the limitations of his space. He re-formed the existing elements and gave his ideas of harmonious proportion a completely new application.

The close relationship in which this tangible illusionism stood with the art of relief sculpture is clearly demonstrated in the facade decorations by Tullio Lombardo for the Scuola di San Marco in Venice.

Walking over the bridge to the church of SS. Giovanni e Paolo, one sees to the left the facade of the Scuola di San Marco. One is then at exactly the right distance from the front of the building to be convinced that the facade is broken by a gallery to either side of the two entrances (Plates 30, 31). In actuality, the impression is created by a series of reliefs fashioned by the Venetian sculptor about 1490. The reliefs that flank the principal entrance show a barrel-vaulted space in which stand the lions of St. Mark. The fictive galleries at the sides of the other entrance have coffered ceilings. To left and right are scenes in relief of the life of St. Mark: the healing and baptism of Anianus.[3]

It is difficult to believe that Lombardo could have achieved this integration of relief sculpture and real and illusionary architecture without being familiar with Bramante's choir.

Smaller architectural elements in distorted perspective also offered solutions for aesthetic problems. Antonio da Sangallo the Younger, a pupil of Bramante, began in 1534 to work on the Palazzo Farnese for Pope Paul III (Michelangelo completed the upper story of the building after Sangallo's death).[4] From the principal entrance a large hall, in plan like the body of a basilica, leads to an interior court (Fig. 19). The wide central aisle is covered with a barrel vault supported by columns. The passages to either side are distinctly narrower and higher than the central one, and they have flat ceilings.

The proportions and position of the lateral passages do not correspond with the arcades that surround the inner court. In order to bring about a harmonious transition between these parts, Sangallo enlarged the entrances to the lateral passages by means of an illusionistic relief in perspective. The rectangular openings with their little lunettes were given the correct proportions by canting the wall surface and adding fan-shaped reliefs with radiating coffers (Plate 33). The illusion is not completely successful. It is best observed when one sees the whole from an oblique frontal position. The resemblance to Bramante's choir is, however, unmistakable.

The three examples of architectural illusionism just discussed are all based on relief sculpture. Through systematic deformation of familiar architectural details within a limited space, the impression is created that the wall is actually extended. Toward the end of the sixteenth century, another element came to the fore. The painters of stage scenery did not stop at using perspective on a flat surface or in a relief. By precipitously reducing the scale of their backgrounds from that of real forms and real spaces, they could

*Fig. 19* Palazzo Farnese, Rome. Groundplan (after Létarouilly)

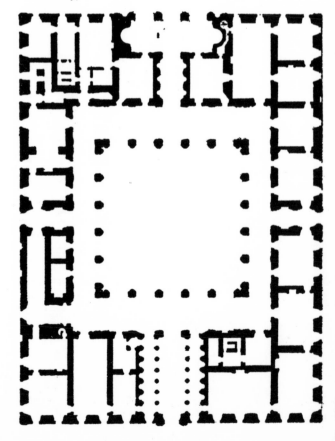

create the effect of deep city views in a very narrow space behind the stage. Later, architects adopted this principle in the world-as-theater mood of the seventeenth century.

The most famous early example of this illusionistic scenographic architecture is Andrea Palladio's last work: the Teatro Olimpico in Vicenza. The semicircular theater, built after a Roman prototype, has a proscenium richly decorated with statuary. Five passageways lead out from the rear of the stage to the *prospettiva*, or distant view—streets of wood that climb obliquely and quickly become narrower, with wooden facades on both sides that rapidly diminish in size toward the back of the stage (Fig. 20). Certainly the perspective here has been helped a little (Plate 36).

Today it is considered unlikely that Palladio designed this frivolity. It is generally attributed to Vincenzo Scamozzi, who completed the building after Palladio's death.[5]

If it is possible to enlarge the apparent size of a space through the manipulation of volumes and lines, the opposite is also possible. By controlling natural perspective, a faraway object can be brought closer.

When Michelangelo was commissioned in 1538 to remodel the piazza and buildings on the Capitoline Hill in Rome, his options were very limited. The Palazzo Senatorio, which borders the piazza at the rear, as seen from the stairs, makes an angle of 80 degrees with the Palazzo dei Conservatori on the right. Here again a limitation of possible choices provided the stimulus for an ingenious invention. For the lefthand side of the hilltop, Michelangelo designed a companion piece to the Palazzo dei Conservatori that would form the same acute angle with the Senator's Palace (Fig. 21). (This palace—the Palazzo Capitolino or Palazzo Nuovo—was not built until the seventeenth century.)

The result is a happy and effective one. Having climbed the broad stairway to the Campidoglio, one sees the Palazzo Senatorio dominating the piazza from the far end, for the receding lines of the flanking palace facades pull it optically into the foreground (Plate 29).

St. Peter's Square in Rome offers the visitor a similarly dramatic experience. The semicircular colonnades by Bernini (1656–57) that bracket the forecourt of St. Peter's church are connected with the front of the church by straight corridors (Fig. 22, Plate 28). The facade, in any case imposing, is set off and made overwhelming.

When one enters the corridor on the right, the passage seems to continue on unchecked. But behind a dramatic fall of light with a hidden light source, the corridor ends in a stairway—the Scala Regia—built by Bernini in 1663–66 (Plate 32).

Here, too, the commission involved redesigning—in this case, an existing stairway with an irregular form that became narrower as it rose. The area between St. Peter's and the Vatican palaces was fixed in this form, and Bernini could do no more than compensate for these irregularities; in this he was successful. He con-

*Fig. 20* Teatro Olimpico, Vicenza. Groundplan

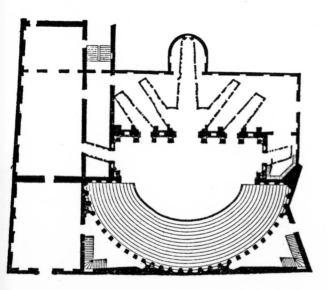

*Fig. 21* The Campidoglio, Rome. Groundplan

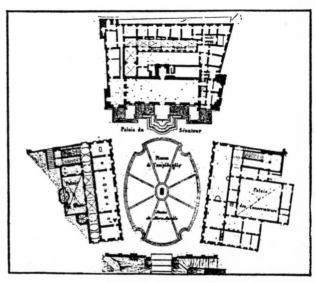

73

cealed the stair walls with a row of columns; those at the top of the Scala Regia are closer to the walls than those below (Plates 34, 35). This device at least partially counteracts the narrowing effect, as does the addition of a landing halfway up. Nevertheless, the difference in width at the top remains visible from below. Bernini used a restrained form of accelerated perspective and added another theatrical effect: the contrast between light and dark.

The connection between architecture and theatrical scenery is much clearer in Francesco Borromini's well-known colonnade in the Palazzo Spada, of about 1635 (Plates 37–41). Sometime after 1632, Borromini received a commission from Cardinal Bernardino Spada to beautify his palace. Off the central court the

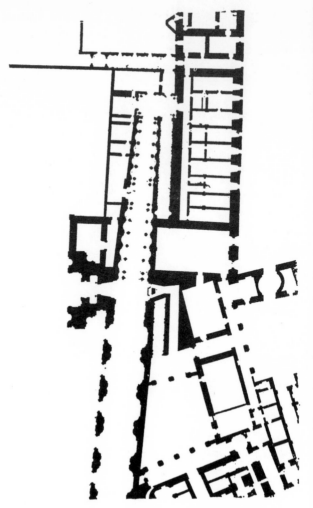

Fig. 23 Scala Regia, The Vatican. Groundplan

Fig. 22 St. Peter's and St. Peter's Square, The Vatican. Planimetric drawing (after Cipriani)

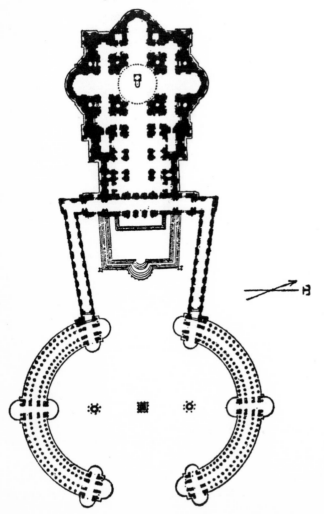

architect built a colonnade which has never missed its effect on the visitor's powers of imagination. At first glance, a long colonnaded corridor (which appears to be some 40 yards deep) leads into another interior court. The entrance (the corona and the out-of-scale consoles were added later) is 18 feet 8 inches (5.68 meters) high and 10 feet 3 inches (3.12 meters) wide; on the other side, however—28 feet 2 inches (8.58 meters) away—the measurements are reduced to 8 feet (2.45 meters) and 3 feet 3 inches (1 meter) respectively. The architecture here serves only to create a visual impression. At the same time it is still a real passage, leading nevertheless into a blind court. Reality thus becomes theater.[6]

All these manipulations of visual experience have much in common with anamorphosis, and not only with regard to construction. (The retarded perspective of the Campidoglio and St. Peter's Square in Rome is even the same in principle.) The main point is that there is a difference between objective reality and the impression that the subjective viewer is to have of it.

The exemplar of accelerated perspective dates from the Late Baroque period. To house a precious relic, the shroud of Christ, the Duke of Milan commissioned Guarino Guarini to design a chapel (1668–94). Guarini, who was bewitched by mathematics and complex geometric figures, crowned the chapel with an enchanting dome (Plate 42). He placed wreaths of windows over each other; from within, the effect is of interwoven polygons that intersect and overlap (Plate 43). Because the size of these polygons keeps decreasing toward the top of the dome, although they retain their shape, the impression is created of a light-shaft high over the chapel (Fig. 25).

This mysterious space bathes in a flood of diffuse, indirect light that falls through invisible openings. Over all soars the Holy Ghost in the form of a white dove, surrounded by a golden wreath of rays and a star.[7]

*Fig. 24* Borromini's colonnade in the Palazzo Spada, Rome. Groundplan

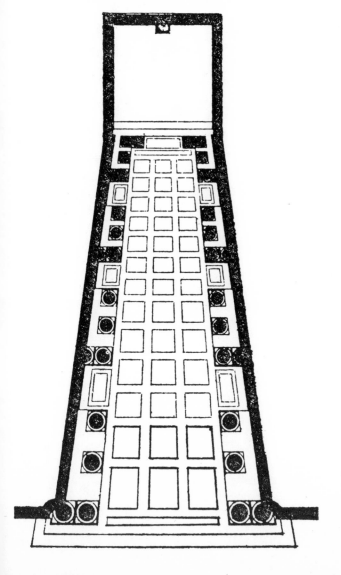

Notes

1  O. Förster, *Bramante* (Vienna–Munich, 1956), pp. 77–78.

2  *Ibid.*, p. 97.

3  L. Planiscig, *Venezianische Bildhauer der Renaissance* (Vienna, 1921), p. 229.

4  H. Siebenhüner, "Der Palazzo Farnese in Rom," *Wallraf-Richartz-Jahrbuch* 14 (1952): 144–64.

5  G. Zorzi, *Le Ville e i teatri di Andrea Palladio* (Vicenza, 1969), pp. 294–97.

6  E. Hempel, *Francesco Borromini* (Vienna, 1924), pp. 49–50.

7  M. Passanti, *Nel mondo magico di Guarino Guarini* (Turin, 1963), pp. 163–94.

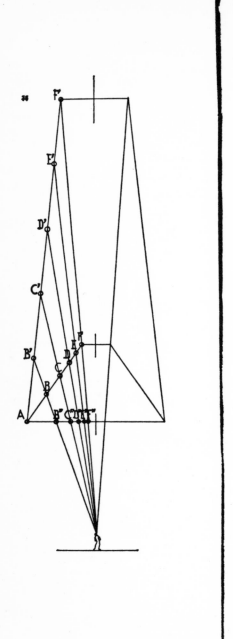

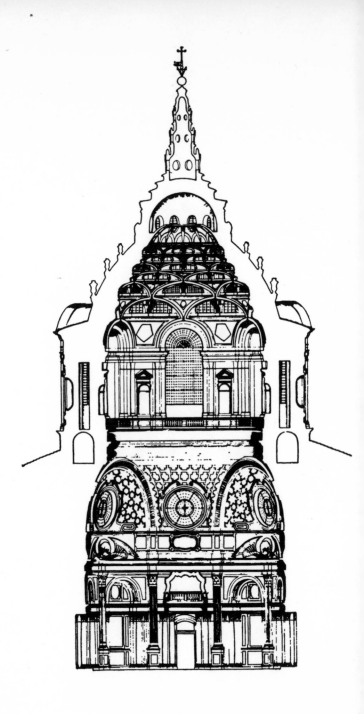

*Fig. 25* Dome of S. Sindone, Turin. Cross section and schematic drawing (after Passanti)

Led astray by the uniform shape of the architectural elements, we tend to imagine that they are also all of equal size. If they were, the actual surface "A–B–C–D–E–F" would become "A´–B´–C´–D´–E´–F´."

*Captions to the following plates are on page 81*

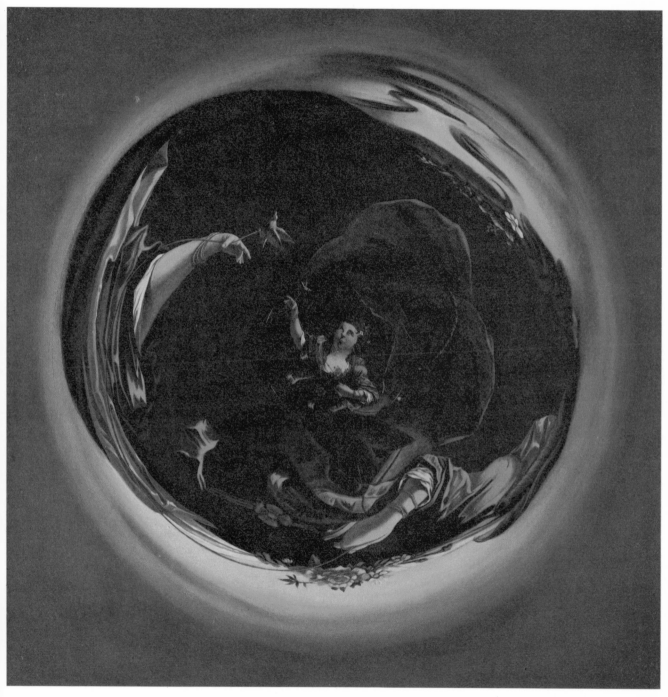

60

61

62 ▷

63

64

65

66

*To the plates on pages 77–80*

59 Henry Kettle. Cone anamorphosis: *A Girl with a Bird on a String*. c. 1770. Oil on panel, 27 ⅛ x 26 ¾" (69 x 68 cm). Collection Schuyt, Amsterdam

The construction of a painting for the reflecting cone was explained by Vaulezard, Niceron, and DuBreuil (Fig. 33). Yet, so far as can be determined, no example survives from the seventeenth century. The particular properties of the cone anamorphosis are fascinatingly expressed in this example. The original composition is turned completely inside out. The girl's face is blurred on the outer rim. In the painting the blue sky is encircled by the girl's body, yet in the reflection it is the sky that encircles her. The girl's arms in the painting dangle inward like tentacles, and the string attached to the bird, which looks as though it were being captured from the sky, describes a protracted curve.

60, 61 Anonymous Netherlandish. Cone anamorphoses: *Clover Leaf*. Eighteenth century. Etchings, colored, 10½ x 10½" (26.5 x 26.5 cm). Collection Elffers, Amsterdam

62 *Two Men Boxing* (see caption to Plates 106, 107)

63–66 Details from the ceiling of the corridor to the apartments of Saint Ignatius in Rome (see Plates 22, 23)

# 6. Perspective Cabinets

Samuel van Hoogstraten makes the following observation in Chapter Seven of *Inleyding tot de Hooge Schoole der Schilderkonst* (Introduction to the Advanced School of Painting).

I will pass over the manner in which, through reflected lines, malformed shapes may be restored to their correct aspect in reflecting globes, angled mirrors, and cylinders; for these are truly artifices rather than essential arts. But still, a master must know the principles by which these diversions are created so that he may not—should the occasion arise—find himself in embarrassment when he must paint an oblique-angled, round, or otherwise unusually formed building or vault. However full of angles they are, vaults and walls can be prepared through this art in such a way that they seem to have a completely different shape; indeed, one can almost paint the corners and angled walls away. And, should pictures or narrative paintings be added there, they will exceed all marvels if they are done by someone who has understanding of it.[1]

As an example of this technique of "painting away," Van Hoogstraten selects Giulio Romano's Sala dei Giganti in the Palazzo del Te in Mantua (Plate 20). Apparently Van Hoogstraten does not consider the mirror-anamorphoses that he mentions at the beginning of the passage true art, but as exercises for improving mastery of perspective. The illusionistic paintings that he discusses in connection with anamorphoses are very rare in the Netherlands. As his sole example, Van Hoogstraten mentions a painting by Carel Fabritius in a private house in Delft. He deplores the fact that none of Fabritius's works are to be found in palaces or churches.[2]

A domestic variant of this art form did have a brief flowering in the Netherlands. Countless, indeed, are the paintings of interiors with black-and-white marble floors, views into adjoining rooms, and evocative alternation of light and dark areas. In the fifties and sixties of the seventeenth century, in the hands of the painters of the School of Delft, these pictures enjoyed great popularity. Particularly skilled in this area were Pieter de Hooch and Jan Vermeer—as were also Fabritius and Van Hoogstraten himself. Given their strictly geometrical basis, these formalized settings demanded a thoroughgoing familiarity with perspective.

The other kind of indoor painting—the church interiors by Pieter Jansz Saenredam of Haarlem and later Gerard Houckgeest and Hendrick Cornelisz van Vliet of Delft—required an even greater mastery of projected rendering on a flat surface. The frequent hesitations observable in Saenredam's drawings, when arches are to be shown in foreshortening or border distortions occur that result from slavish adherence to principles of construction show how difficult it is to achieve an acceptable result when one works from lessons learned.

But all of these examples are painted on flat surfaces. Shortly after the passage cited above, Van Hoogstraten mentions the "perspectyfkas," or perspective cabinet, as a product of the "mastery of the art" (that is, of perspective). The astonishing effect of the perspective cabinet, says Van Hoogstraten, is that it "makes a figure the length of your finger appear life-size."

Only a few of these perspective cabinets still exist. In a recently published, comprehensive article by Susan Koslow, only six are mentioned.[3] Curiosities of this kind, including anamorphoses, are particularly vulnerable to the passage of time. When the effect of the first astonishment is over, they are generally consigned to the attic.

The most beautiful of these cabinets—insofar as quality of construction and of painting go—is one made by Van Hoogstraten himself (Plates 67–74). It is a rectangular cabinet with side walls painted on the outside as well as the inside. One long side is not original, and of later date; in its place there was probably once an opening to let in light. There are peepholes on both of the short sides, close to the corners where the long unpainted sides abut (Plates 68–69).

These peepholes are at the horizon line of the perspective construction in the interior. The viewer's sense of scale is thus reduced to that of the pictured furnishings (Plate 74). Moreover, he is obliged to observe the correct distance with regard to the two sides and the lid and base of the cabinet that he can survey from either peephole. The representation fills his whole field of vision, and he can look to left and right, up and down, without having the illusion of a real milieu slip into distortion. Van Hoogstraten created the effect of this illusion in a variety of ways. First of all, there are several open doors that give different outward views. A variety of alternating patterns in the marble floor and a repetition of such similar elements as doorways and chairs pull the eye into depth. The principal points are the corners and the junctures of the painted sides. The central room into which the viewer looks frequently cuts across the actual shape of the cabinet, breaking the relation between the painted surface and the space represented. A few objects in the corners even extend across two or more planes. Seen through the peephole, the little dog seems to sit on a continuous floor, but in reality he is extremely deformed, being painted across a corner, and a chair that looks perfectly sound is actually in three parts (Plates 72, 73).

One effect that cannot be captured in a photograph is made on the lid. Through an anamorphic distortion, the wall seems to run onto the ceiling, and the pictures high on the wall are so distorted that, in accordance with the anamorphic principle, they seem to float free. Above, on the outside of the lid, is a perspective anamorphosis of Venus and Cupid.

Two cabinets by unknown makers in Copenhagen's Nationalmuseum fall into the simplest category of perspective boxes. Both still have their original cases, which have trompe l'oeil decoration, a peephole, and an opening for light. One shows the interior of a Protestant church (Plates 76–78), the other of a Catholic church (Plates 79–81). The construction in each case consists of two walls placed at an acute angle to each other. Only these sides are painted—the low position of the peephole made it unnecessary to paint the lid.

In the Protestant church scene, the eye first falls on a chair in the foreground on which a Bible rests. As repoussoir, the Catholic piece has a small table on which lie a Bible, a cushion, a rosary, and a crucifix.

Extreme disparity in scale between foreground and background was a well-known method among painters of the Delft School for intensifying the impression of depth (see, for example, Vermeer's *The Letter*). Here it is used as a supplement to other means. Both churches show a view from the middle of the building to the apse. This permits a simple construction in central perspective, which is projected on both surfaces in such a way that through the peephole one sees the distorted forms as normal. Because the painted surfaces are viewed from a corner, the deformation is counteracted. One can look farther to left and right in the Catholic church, as parts of the transept are depicted. The floors with their lines of juncture between the slabs retain the painter's perspective schema.

The churches are intended as types—indeed, seem caricatures of their species. The Protestant church is sparsely furnished with benches, a choir screen, a pulpit, and modestly dressed worshipers. The Catholic interior, on the other hand, teems with altars, the visitors are richly clad, and one of the monks kneels before a pontiff.

In Copenhagen there is another perspective cabinet with an opulent Dutch interior (Plate 82). Its construction is, again, rectangular. The front panel has disappeared. The perspective system is simpler by far than Van Hoogstraten's, for the painter has chosen the easiest approach; in fact, the corners of the represented room coincide with those of the box almost exactly.

The creator of a perspective cabinet in the Bredius Museum in The Hague used his options much more cleverly (Plates 90–96). As with the church interiors, the scene is constructed on two surfaces, which, in this case, make a right angle with each other. Here, however, the upper and lower surfaces have also been painted, and this enabled the artist to make his very symmetrical composition more lively. Unless one looks at the scene from the right point of view, the raftered ceiling seems to break at the places where the sides of the box meet, and the rear wall, too, looks as though it had been pinched into a fold. The rendering of the chair in the foreground is extremely artful.

A similar level of expertise is displayed in a cabinet in Detroit that is pentagonal in construction (Plates 83–89). The huge pillars in the hall bypass the discontinuous picture plane entirely, and the charming still life in the foreground contains a plate that also extends over three surfaces. The cat that stares the viewer directly in the eye is an amusing touch; the dog excitedly attacking him is painted in the immediate foreground on the floor of the box. The words "memento mori" are written over the door, and on the table is a pocket watch on a ribbon. This whole shadow world is itself reflected in the shining ball over the inscription.

Notes

1   Samuel van Hoogstraten, *Inleyding tot de Hooge Schoole der Schilderkonst* (Rotterdam, 1678), p. 274.
2   *Ibid.*, p. 275.

3   S. Koslow, "De wonderlijke Perspectyfkas: An Aspect of Seventeenth-Century Dutch Painting," *Oud Holland* 82 (1967): 35–56.

# 7. Sixteenth - Century Perspective Anamorphoses

Holbein's sojourn in England left behind some anamorphic traces. His successor as court painter, William Scrots, is the probable author of one of the best-known anamorphoses.[1] This horizontal oil in the National Portrait Gallery in London (Plate 1) is a distorted profile portrait painted in an elongated oval inscribed with figures and letters. A landscape borders the portrait, and on the right there is a hollow in the frame.

The first description we have of this curious representation dates from 1584, when Lupold von Wedel saw it at Whitehall. Seen directly from the front, the portrait was so distorted that it was difficult to recognize the face as human. But a metal rod with a little disk on it had been attached to the painting. One had to pull this out to a distance of about 26 inches (66 centimeters), and when one then looked through the hole in the disk, "the ugly face was transformed into a handsomely proportioned countenance."[2]

The sighting device Von Wedel mentions has disappeared, but he gives a clear description as to how such paintings were viewed. Seen from the correct position, a profile portrait of Edward VI appeared in a medallion. The inscription around the border states his age, nine years, and the year the portrait was painted, 1546. The landscape encircling the picture can be dated about 1600. Before this addition was made, by a Flemish artist, the background was probably dark, which would have heightened the anamorphic effect of the central image.

Erhard Schön's picture puzzles stimulated considerable popularity for perspective anamorphoses in southern Germany. An unusual painting now in Milan shows, at first glance, a landscape reminiscent of Hieronymus Bosch (Plate 4). The fantastic, distorted forms have a distinctly disquieting aura. At the bottom is a recognizable landscape with several small figures engaged in trapping birds with nets. At bottom right an indistinct face swims into view. In the middle of the landscape there suddenly emerges a batlike creature with dangling bells and wings full of eyes. At the upper border, the scene becomes more peaceful and a new landscape with a ship and a rabbit hunt unfolds.

Several peepholes have been bored into the frame on both sides. As with Schön's largest woodcut, one has to look alternately from left and right to discover the true nature of the painting, for beneath these curiosities are concealed religious representations. Thus, you must look from a sharp angle first to the left and then to the right in the upper zone of the picture, where St. Peter and St. Paul and then Christ and the angel of Gethsemane will appear. The little sailboat and its sturdy oarsmen are now recognizable as Christ's goblet. The monstrous creature below dissolves into the veil of St. Veronica, viewed from the right, and the Madonna and Child also spring into view from this angle. The forms here are so distorted that they are rendered completely unrecognizable. The little lake at the lower border becomes St. Francis of Assisi receiving his stigmata.

Through a clever manipulation of elements from the landscape painting of fantasy and an exuberant exploitation of perspective distortion, the anonymous painter created one of the most fascinating examples of anamorphic art. He probably made it about the middle of the sixteenth century.[3]

North of the Alps, the tradition originally inspired by Schön persisted into the seventeenth century. One ingenious copperplate engraving by Johann Heinrich Glaser, an artist from Basel, dated May 24, 1638, is dedicated in an inscription to Remigius Fäsch, Chancellor of the University of Basel (Fig. 26). The elongated and unintelligible pattern of lines that fills the center is surrounded by a representation of paradise. To the right, the Fall of Man is depicted: Here, Eve is seen handing Adam the apple in a landscape filled with cleverly drawn animals. At the opposite side again are Adam and Eve, with Death as companion, driven out of paradise by an angel with a

*Fig. 26* Johann Heinrich Glaser. Perspective anamorphosis: *Christ with the Crown of Thorns, Flanked on the Right by the Fall from Grace and on the Left by the Expulsion from Paradise.* 1639 . Engraving

In this engraving—viewed diagonally from the right—the suffering Christ appears in the middle of the landscape of paradise. His unseen presence during the commission of the original sin has religious significance. From the inscription one learns that this picture was dedicated to Remigius Fäsch, Chancellor of the University of Basel. Three cylindrical anamorphoses in the Historisches Museum, Basel, are also by Glaser (Plates 137, 138).

flaming sword. When the picture is observed obliquely from the right, Christ as Man of Sorrows with a crown of thorns appears in the center.

In this engraving, anamorphic form has acquired new theological meaning. The events of the first chapter of Genesis (the birth of original sin) find their fulfillment in the sufferings of Christ, who offers man the opportunity to redeem himself from his wickedness. From a heavenly perspective, he is even present at the scene of the Fall.

In Chapter One, we mentioned the influence of Leonardo's invention; the northern Italians seem to have become particularly interested in anamorphosis. Even before Giovanni Paolo Lomazzo's treatise of 1584, the first guide to the construction of perspective anamorphoses appeared there. Daniele Barbaro mentions in his *Pratica della Prospettiva* of 1569 two methods that had already been rudimentarily explored by Leonardo: one empiric and the other geometric.[4]

The first method requires that a representation of some object, for example a face, be drawn in the normal way on a sheet of paper. The lines of the drawing must then be perforated with rather large holes. Then the drawing is held with one side at right angles to the wall on which the image is to be painted. One allows either sunlight or the light from a lamp to stream through the holes onto the wall, where an elongated form appears, which is traced. When one examines the copied form from the spot where the light originated, the face is visible again just as it was on the paper. (Unfortunately, when sunlight is used to cast the image, insurmountable difficulties occur; Barbaro clearly made an error here.)

Barbaro indicated that he would provide a geometrical approach, too, but this promise he does not keep. But he does emphasize that the picture may be concealed by submerging it in a landscape.

Lomazzo deals at length with the construction of anamorphoses by the geometrical method. In Chapter Twenty, Book Six, of his treatise, he describes a "method of making an inverted perspective that looks correct when it is observed through a single peephole."

"You must," he begins, "place a piece of canvas or board on the wall of a colonnade. It must be fifteen braccias long [about 29 feet 6 inches, or 9 meters]—slightly more or less, as you please—and one braccia high [about 2 feet, or 60 centimeters]. Fasten it to the wall. Then, on the same side of the wall, attach a handsomely designed horse or a head of Christ, or whatever you wish to paint, in a frame. It must be covered with a grid of horizontal and vertical lines. This painting must be exactly as high as the board and must be fastened on one side to the wall next to the edge of the board. You must then move backwards far enough so that the board attached to the wall is screened by the frame that you have just moved away from and which projects from the wall. Be sure to stand at a considerable distance from the frame, with your eye exactly opposite the center of it: that is, so that its 'optica' [the central axis of the visual pyramid] is precisely centered on the frame. Then extend out

from your eye, or the place where it is, a string with which you will transfer to the board all the squares that are drawn in the frame; they must be copied there."[5]

In the distended network of lines that results, the model-picture is traced by using a very long cane, at the end of which a piece of charcoal is fastened.

The horse and the head of Christ that Lomazzo gives as examples were mentioned in Chapter One. Unfortunately, nothing remains of these monumental compositions. Such material as has survived from the sixteenth century is small in size, probably intended for private use. One of these small pieces from northern Italy shows a landscape, loosely painted, filled with charming figures in the Late Mannerist style of Niccolò dell'Abate.[6] The motifs are intermingled in a curious way (Plate 45). To the right, St. Jerome kneels before a crucifix by a cliff, while in the foreground herdsmen picnic and a flute player gazes quietly out at us. To the left, a small group of people are swimming in a little lake. Those familiar with anamorphoses will pick out the hidden images at once. Yet the Baptism of Christ is not woven very convincingly into the cliff wall, and the head of John the Baptist on a platter (the small lake) is intelligible only in conjunction with the baptismal scene. The picture's charm does not lie in the success with which the secondary layer of content is concealed. The contrast between lightheartedness and deadly seriousness gives it its ironic flavor.

Notes

1   R. Strong, *Catalogue of the National Portrait Gallery: Tudor and Jacobean Portraits* (London, 1969), vol. 1, pp. 88–90.

2   *Ibid.*

3   J. Baltrušaitis, *Anamorphoses* (Paris, 1969), p. 29.

4   *Ibid.*, pp. 34–35.

5   G. P. Lomazzo, *Trattato dell'arte della pittura* (Rome, 1844), vol. 2, pp. 174–75.

6   J. Baltrušaitis, *op. cit.*, pp. 26–29.

67–74 Samuel van Hoogstraten. Perspective cabinet: *Dutch Interior.* c. 1655–60. Rectangular base, 22⅞ x 34⅝ x 25″ (58 x 88 x 63.5 cm). National Gallery, London

The perspective rendering of a room with many outward vistas is projected on five painted surfaces (Plate 67). Peepholes have been bored in the side walls. If one looks through either of these holes, one receives the impression of a continuous space (Plates 68, 69). Because the viewing angle from which one observes the surfaces is differential, Van Hoogstraten occasionally used severe anamorphic distortions (Plates 70, 71). Seen through the peephole, the proportions once more appear normal; also, the spatial illusion is greater in these instances because the objects negate the flatness of the surface on which they are painted.

75 Carel Fabritius. *A View in Delft with the Booth of a Seller of Musical Instruments.* 1652. Oil on canvas, 6 x 12⅞″ (15.4 x 31.6 cm). National Gallery, London

Because of the remarkable spatial illusion created by the curved lines and the extreme difference in scale between the foreground and the background, it is assumed that this small painting was meant to be observed through a peephole—just like a perspective cabinet—or was even actually part of a perspective cabinet.

76–78 Anonymous north Netherlandish. Perspective cabinet: *Interior of a Protestant Church.* c. 1660. Triangular base, two side walls each 46⅞ x 29½″ (119 x 75 cm). Nationalmuseet, Copenhagen

The original cases of this box and its companion (Plates 79–81) have been preserved. On the front there is a *trompe l'oeil* painting (Plate 76). Through the peephole one sees the interior of a Dutch church (Plate 77). The joinings of the flagstones draw the eye into the distance, and the impression of depth is accentuated by a chair with a Bible on it, which stands directly in the foreground (Plate 78). When one views the whole without using the peephole, the two side walls remain separate and create a sharp angle.

79–81 Anonymous north Nethlandish. Perspective cabinet: *Interior of a Catholic Church.* c. 1660. Triangular base, two side walls each 46⅞ x 29½″ (119 x 75 cm). Nationalmuseet Copenhagen

This is the Catholic counterpart to the Protestant church shown in Plates 76–78. Here, the painter offers even more charming experiences to beguile the wandering eye, for he painted views into the transepts of the church on the left and right (Plate 81).

82 Anonymous north Netherlandish. Perspective cabinet: *Interior of a Dutch Dwelling.* c. 1670. Rectangular base, 23 x 17¾ x 19¼″ (58.5 x 45 x 49 cm). Nationalmuseet, Copenhagen

In this cabinet little use has been made of the side walls, which form an angle. The corners of the box are almost identical to those of the represented interiors.

83–89 Anonymous north Netherlandish. Perspective cabinet: *View of a Pillared Hall.* 1663. Pentagonal base, 16⅜ x 13½ x 11¼″ (41.9 x 34.5 x 28.6 cm). Detroit Institute of Arts

The artist (possibly Van Hoogstraten) used not only the four perpendicular sides but also the ceiling and the floor. He had no difficulty in showing the soaring pillars running over three sides (Plates 86, 87). The plate in the still life in the foreground is certainly a masterpiece of the art of projection (Plates 84, 85). The dog is in a position to threaten the cat, although they are situated in different dimensions (Plate 88).

90–96 Anonymous, School of Delft. Perspective cabinet. c. 1670. Triangular base, 33⅛ x 32¼ x 23⅝″ (84 x 82 x 60 cm). Bredius Museum, The Hague

The two side walls of this "Perspectyfkas" create a right angle together. If one does not look at the cabinet from the proper viewpoint, many distortions occur. Originally there must have been another wall on the front side, with a peephole. If one finds the right viewpoint, all the surfaces take their place in one perspective system. This is most clearly seen in the raftered ceiling and in the chair in the foreground. The illusion of space is stronger here than in an ordinary painting, the eye can swoop and dart about. The painter took advantage of this by painting vistas on both sides. The tile floor and the ceiling also draw the eye into depth.

67

68

69

70

71

74 ▷

72

73

75

76

77

78

79

80

86

87

88

89

90

93

94

95

96

# 8. Developments During the Seventeenth Century

Because so few seventeenth-century anamorphoses have survived, we can give only a general overview of the most important areas of activity. During this period a number of French mathematicians played a vital role, propounding methods of construction and sometimes realizing them in practical experiments. Furthermore, they considerably increased the variety of the genre. Anamorphoses for reflecting cylinders were introduced, apparently in response to Chinese examples, and soon complicated anamorphoses for reflecting cones were being described. During the 1700s, the latter were to become very popular.[1]

Still other variants of the perspective anamorphosis were the cones and cylinders designed to be painted on the inside as well as the outside. The special rooms that were to have been filled with these fascinating objects were never carried beyond the design stage, but we have illustrations of them in a book by one of these versatile Frenchmen.

Cylindrical anamorphoses must have found their way to Holland, Germany, England, and Scandinavia very early. The few surviving examples of this art in the North must serve as indication of all that was done there.

## Curious Perspectives

The most important work—a large part of which is devoted to anamorphosis—was written by a member of the Order of Minims, Jean-François Niceron, who lived from 1613 to 1646. *La Perspective curieuse* was published during his lifetime, in 1638, and was republished in 1646, after his death, in more extensive form under the title *Thaumaturgus Opticus*.

The method he describes for constructing perspective anamorphoses is purely geometrical. Basically, it is in no way distinguished from traditional perspective construction.

We saw in Chapter Two that, to check for accuracy, Alberti used a diagonal line drawn through the points where horizontal and vertical lines intersected on his foreshortened "chessboard pavement." If such a line ran through the opposite corners of a diagonal sequence of squares, the projection had been correctly made. It was soon discovered that the distance between the points where these diagonals intersect the horizon and the vanishing point is the same as the distance between the eye of the viewer and the vanishing point. Such diagonals make an angle of 45 degrees with the picture plane. Thus we can make a general rule: All lines that make an angle of 45 degrees with the picture plane run into the so-called distance point. This fact simplified the construction of perspective considerably.[2] In order to obtain the correct diminution in distance between lines running papallel to the picture plane, one has only to draw a line from a selected distance point through the bundle of lines that run toward and meet in the vanishing point. Horizontal lines then drawn at the resulting points of intersection will be correctly spaced.

Niceron's diagram is merely an extreme example of this construction (Fig. 27). Rotate the drawing at the bottom (XXXV) 45 degrees and you see the diagonal line construction. "P" is the vanishing point and "R" is the distance point. It is exceptional only because the proportions are very different. The distance point "R" lies close to vanishing point "P," with the result that the projected square is extremely distorted.

Seen from "R," this picture plane becomes illusory. It hangs somewhere in the space behind the surface area and no longer coincides with it. A picture located on the plane "A–B–C–D" (and which is also constructed according to the rules of perspective) would become just as deformed, so that from viewpoint "R" it would give the impression of being mounted on the illusory picture plane (Fig. 28). The result is that the cross section through the visual pyramid has become

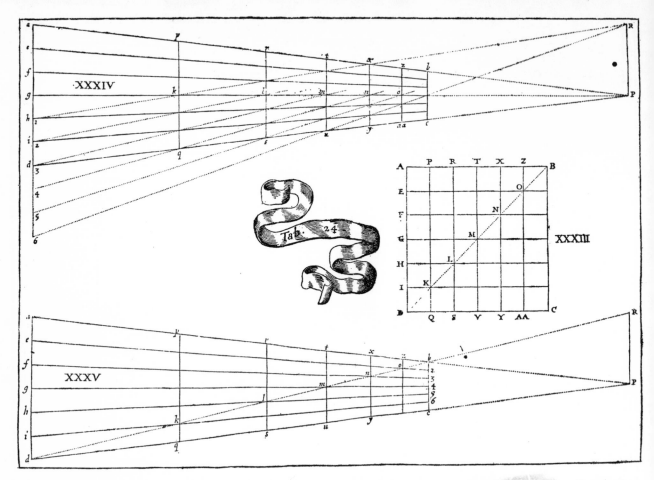

*Fig. 27 (above)* Jean-François Niceron. *Thaumaturgus Opticus . . .* (Rome, 1646), illus. 24

The rectangle XXXIII can, by geometric means, be transformed into an anamorphic rectangle. If one looks at XXXIV and XXXV from viewpoint RP, the original rectangle appears, seemingly released from the paper.

*Fig. 28 (below)* Jean-François Niceron. Perspective anamorphosis: *Saint John on Patmos. Thaumaturgus Opticus . . .* (Rome, 1646), illus. 33

Niceron, who wrote the first extensive guide to anamorphoses, belonged to the same Order as Maignan (see Plates 46–50). This engraving is all that remains of a work he created twice, once in Rome (1642), once in Paris (1644).

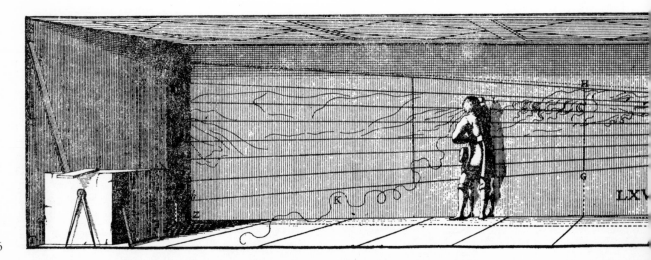

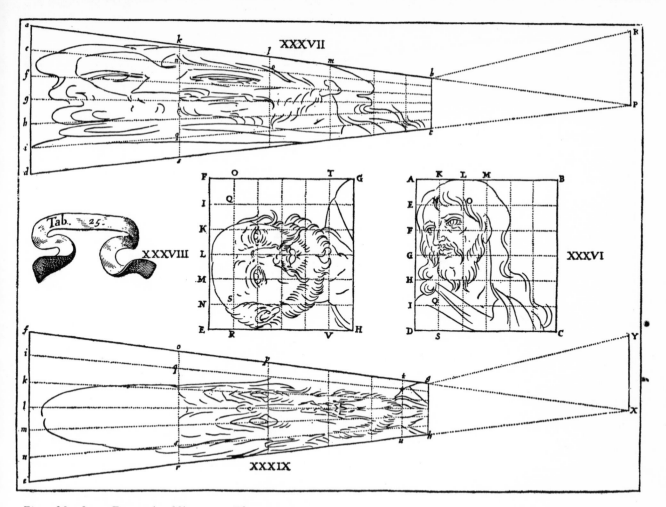

Fig. 29 Jean-François Niceron. *Thaumaturgus Opticus* . . . (Rome, 1646), illus. 25

The projection of a screen or grid in anamorphic perspective makes the transfer of a representation possible.

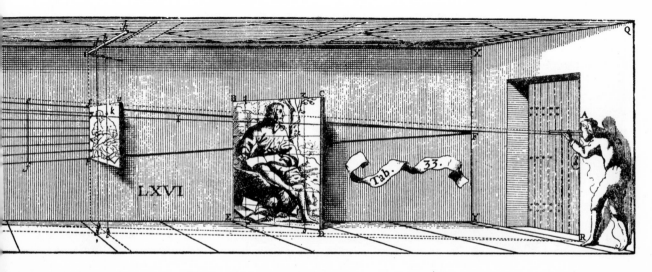

illusory. One can actually visualize it at any arbitrary point between "a–d" and "b–c." In making a construction, this fact is turned to use. The original is then constructed on "b–c."

All of this is reminiscent of Leonardo's mixture of natural and artificial perspective (see pages 25 – 27).

The method Niceron used to make his construction is much like that of Lomazzo (Fig. 29). The original "B–C–E–D" is divided into rectangular fields, and from viewpoint "A" a grid is projected on the wall. The original painting is hinged to the wall where the grid begins ("f–t"). A bar with two plumblines is hung over it. On one of these lines, a sliding plumb ("K") can be fastened at any desired height. The lines can also be pushed here and there across the bar. With these two "coordinates," any point on the original can be established. The painting is then folded back, and from viewpoint "A" a string, "I," is stretched along line "K." The place where the string touches the wall ("L") is marked. The most important points of the original are traced in this fashion. The grid makes a frame for the whole transfer.

This method was very time-consuming, of course, but it represented a practical improvement over Lomazzo's cane and piece of charcoal. It also made possible the execution of various things in larger scale.

Niceron executed the picture illustrated in Figure 29 twice—first in Rome and then, in 1644, in Paris, at the monastery of the Minims in the Place Royale.

Niceron probably invented his apparatus with the help of Emmanuel Maignan, professor of theology at the monastery of SS. Trinità dei Monti in Rome. Maignan was a mathematician and specialist in sundials. One of his largest and most complicated grids for measuring time is found in a passage on the upper floor of the monastery. When you go around the corner from this passage, you enter another hall; here, on one wall, is a gigantic fresco painted in tones of black, gray, and white (Plates 47–50).

An elongated landscape filled with a meaningless pattern of lines and billowing shapes unfolds across a stretch of almost 66 feet (20 meters). The only recognizable feature is a wide waterway with little towns on both banks. At the end of the passage, you reach a place where the image of St. Francis of Paola, kneeling under a tree, deep in prayer, becomes visible in the distance.

This is the only large perspective anamorphosis still in existence. Niceron mentions it, and the title of the second edition of his book is a play on the sobriquet of Francis of Paola, the founder of the Order of Minims. Because of his miraculous deeds, Francis was called "Thaumaturgus," or "performer of miracles." In Maignan's fresco, one of these wonders is depicted: Saint Francis floats on his cloak over the Straits of Messina.

Maignan wrote a book on sundials, *Perspectiva horaria*, published in 1648 in Rome. It includes an engraving that explains the method he employed in constructing his fresco (Plate 46). In general terms, this coincided with what Niceron was doing in 1642 in the passage across the way. Maignan did not, however, use a grid of lines. The original composition was projected directly on the wall.

To the monks of the order, Maignan's fresco probably seemed a kind of synthetic miracle: Through God's natural laws, man is able to create visions. With his normal earthly powers of observation, he can detect nothing but chaos; but from a point determined by natural law, the vision of a saint emerges.

Niceron was in contact with Descartes, who lived for a time in the monastery at the Place Royale. Niceron's interest in anamorphosis and Descartes's abiding concern with the kind of illusion in which reality and observation are disassociated have been seen as interconnected.[3]

Descartes was also interested in the work of Salomon de Caus, who devoted three chapters of his *Perspectiva* (published in 1612 and 1624) to the construction of anamorphoses. His book, however, was less influential than Niceron's.

The technique of projecting a grid on a picture surface is very reminiscent of the methods of the *quadratura* painters as Pozzo describes them. The diagonal construction used in conjunction with it presupposes familiarity with the fact that certain diagonals terminate in a distance point. Leonardo knew the distance-point method, but one can only guess from his anamorphic sketches that he established his grid with a diagonal. It is extremely probable, however, that he did. A sketch of about 1540 by an unknown master, "HR," probably from Nuremberg, displays the diagonal clearly, but it gives no indication of a distance point. By this time, distance-point construction was apparently so commonplace that it was not particularly necessary to note the point.

It was Niceron who firmly established the ground rules for procedure and, with Maignan, invented a practical technique for dealing with large wall surfaces. In his *Thaumaturgus Opticus*, he demonstrates still other kinds of perspective anamorphosis. He proposes a method for painting portraits on cones and

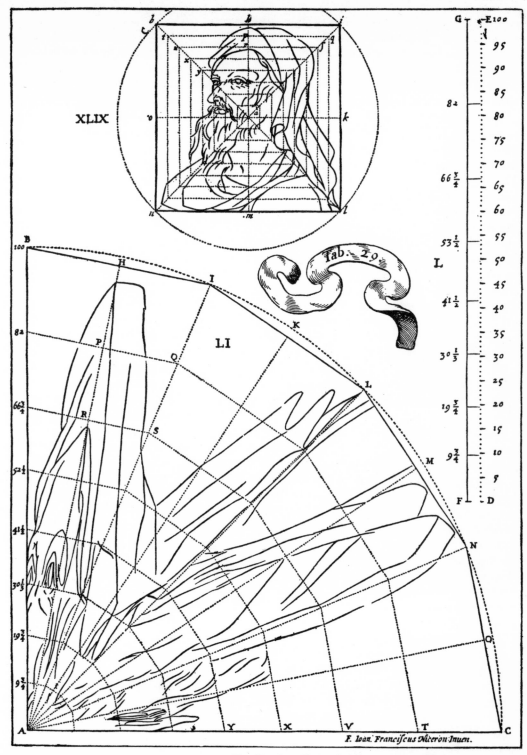

*Fig. 30* Jean-François Niceron. Pyramidal anamorphosis.
*Thaumaturgus Opticus* . . . (Rome, 1646), illus. 29

In drawing LI one can see a flattened pyramid which,
reconstructed and viewed from the apex, should yield the
picture in XLIX.

pyramids that are to be viewed at a fixed distance from their apexes (Fig. 30). As illustration, he added a chart with which the increasing intervals between the concentric rings and squares can be calculated. Properly speaking, these are three-dimensional anamorphoses. Jean DuBreuil, one of Niceron's followers, even conceived of rooms in which conical and pyramidal anamorphoses were to be set up (Fig. 31). These geometrical objects could be painted inside and outside, with base or apex either set on the floor or suspended from the ceiling. Other rooms were designed to be filled with ordinary perspective anamorphoses, which could be looked at horizontally, from below, or from above (Fig. 32).

*Figs. 31, 32* Jean DuBreuil. *La Perspective pratique* . . . (Paris, 1649), pt. 3, pp. 112, 122

In these copper engravings, we see four rooms containing different types of anamorphoses: conical anamorphoses, which may be painted on the interior or the exterior (Fig. 31 *below*); and pyramidal anamorphoses, for which the same holds true (Fig. 31 *above*). Normal perspective anamorphoses can also be viewed from many angles (Fig. 32).

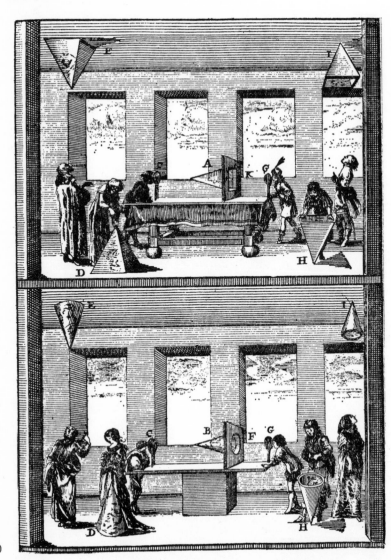

None of these rooms is in existence, but both Niceron and DuBreuil investigated a completely different kind of anamorphosis, which was to exceed all others in popularity.

Reflecting Cones and Cylinders

In a copperplate engraving by Jean Tröschel, after a design by Simon Vouet, a group of astonished satyrs crowd about a striking object. On a table stands a shiny cylinder that reflects the distorted image of an elephant in correct perspective. The engraving must have been made between 1624 and 1627, when Tröschel and Vouet lived in Rome.[4] The optical marvel in the engraving is treated as something completely new and exotic. The elephant suggests a possible Asiatic origin for the idea.

The discovery was publicized for the first time in 1630 in *Perspective cylindrique et conique* by Vaulezard. He shows how images can be distorted with the aid of a grid and then restored to their normal form when they are reflected in a mirror, a cylinder, or a cone. Niceron and DuBreuil also discuss this in their books (Figs. 33, 34). There is scarcely any doubt that the mathematical principles behind the invention were described for the first time in this milieu. But their origin remains obscure.

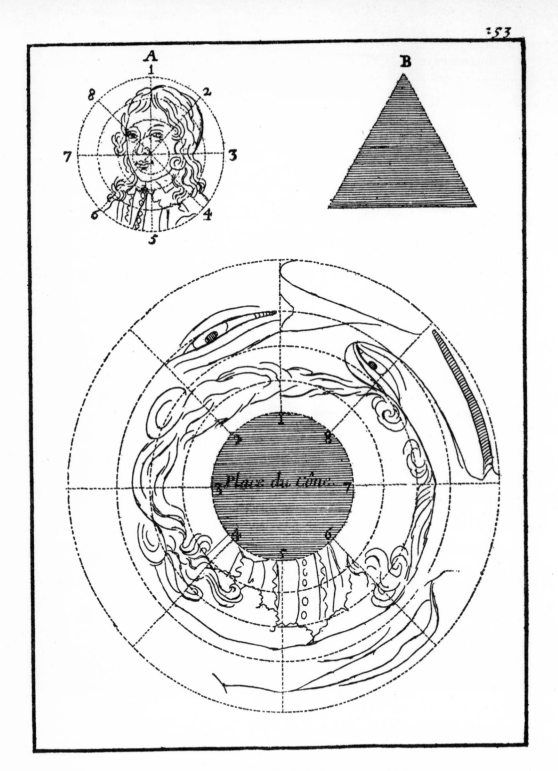

*Fig. 33* Jean DuBreuil. *La Perspective pratique* . . . (Paris, 1649), pt. 3, p. 153

Cone anamorphoses are also prepared by geometric means. By inverting and expanding the original lines, one can "anamorphotize" the original image.

*Captions to the following plates are on pages 129–30*

97

98

99

100

101

102

103

104

105

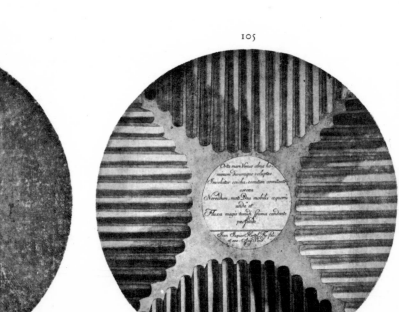

106

107

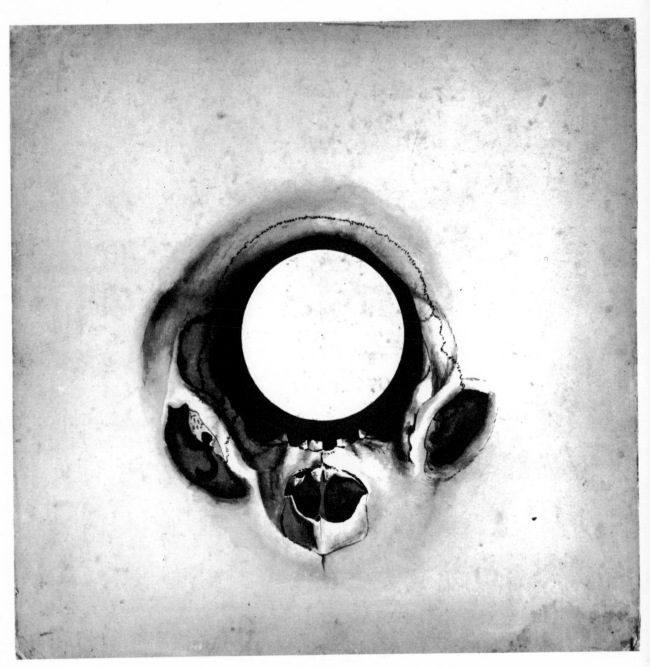

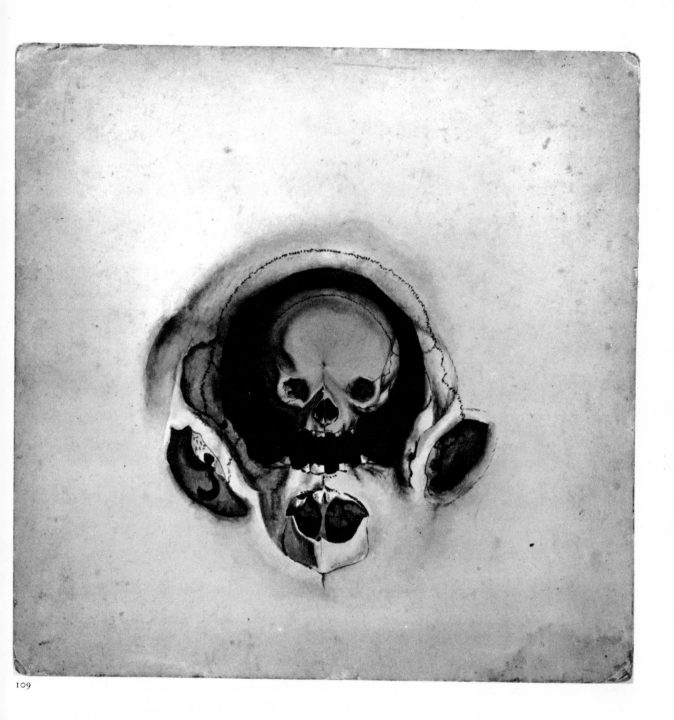

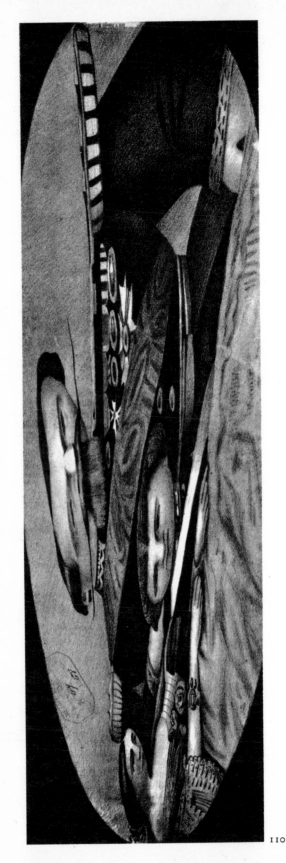

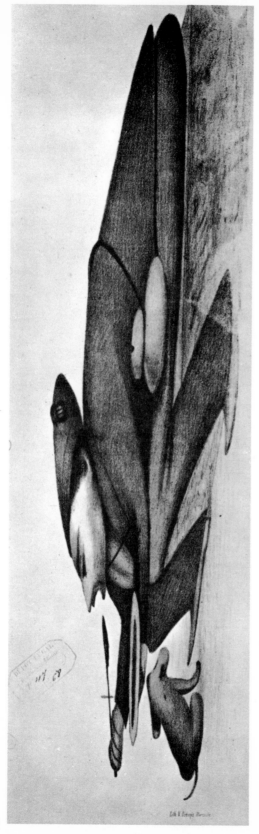

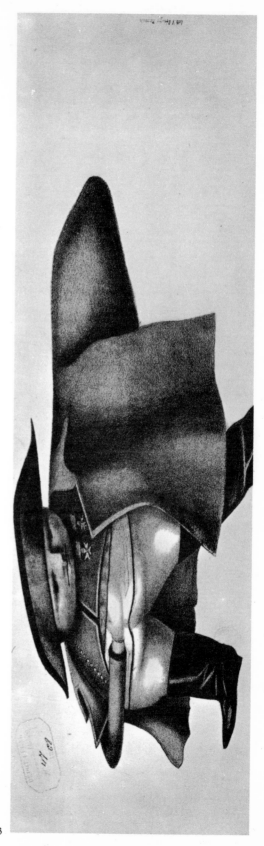

Lith V Bohenia Horvat

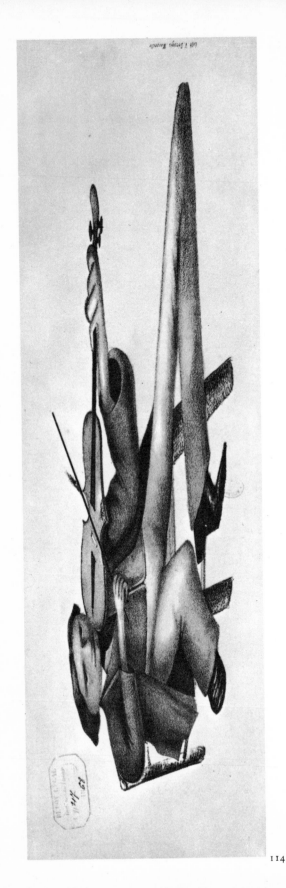

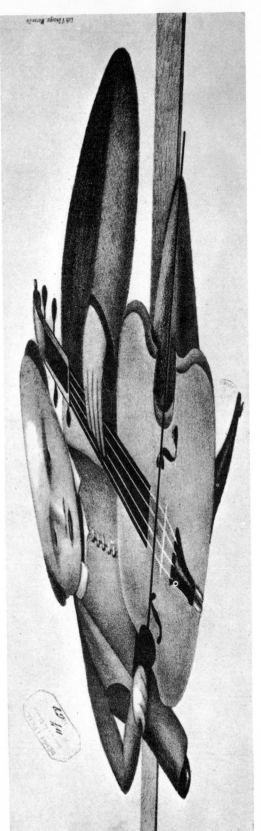

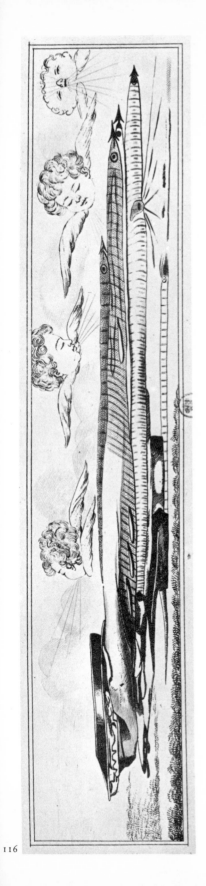

116

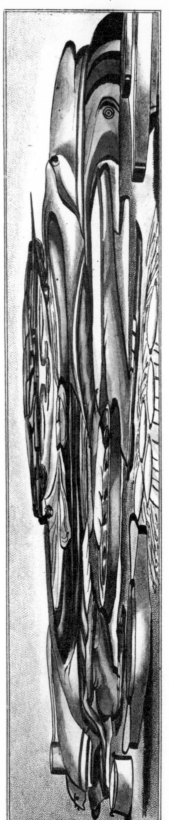

117

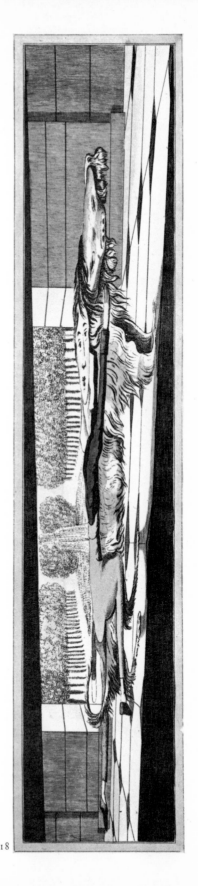

118

120

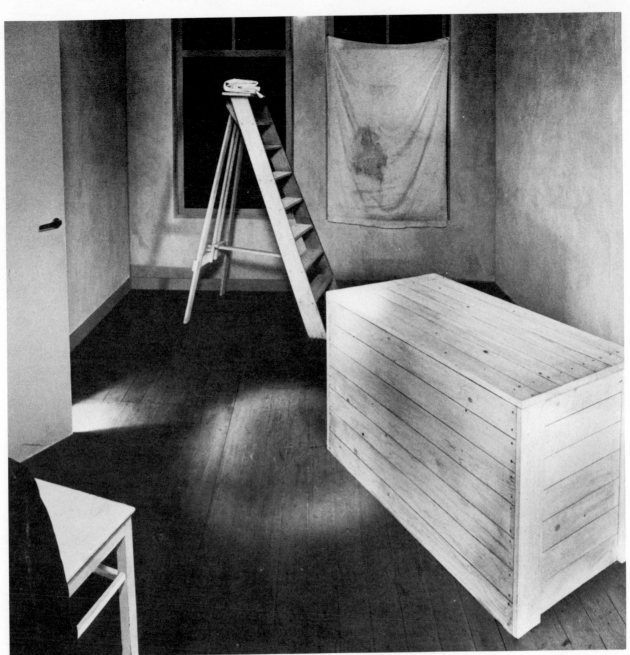

122

123

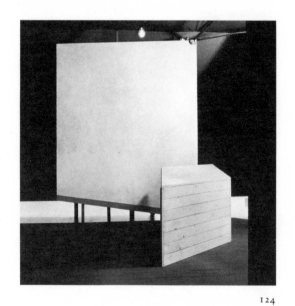

124

125

126

127

97 Henry Kettle. Pyramid anamorphosis: *Four Male Portraits Become One*. c. 1770. Oil on panel, 8¾ x 8¾″ (22.5 x 22.5 cm). Rijksmuseum voor de Geschiedenis der Natuurwetenschappen, Leiden

Henry Kettle probably studied the work of DuBreuil with great care (cf. Fig. 34). The four reflecting surfaces must each encompass one portion of the four heads. He also signed this small painting: "H. Kettle pinxt."

98 James Steere. *H.M.S. "Victory."* 1786. Oil on panel. Science Museum, London

Perhaps influenced by Kettle's work, Steere or another artist reworked this painting of a model of the flagship of the British fleet anamorphically (see Plates 99, 149). The beautiful lines of the ship's hull make it a tempting object for anamorphic distortion.

99–101 See the Game Section, captions to Plates 129, 149, 151

102, 103 Monogramist , Augsburg. Two cone anamorphoses: *Apollo and Marsyas* and *Silenus*. Second half of the eighteenth century. Etching, colored, diameter 10¾″ (27.5 cm) Danske Tekniske Museum, Helsingør

104, 105 Johann Georg Hertel. Two cone anamorphoses: *Four-leafed Clover* and *Seashells*. Second half of the eighteenth century. Etching, colored, diameter 8¾″ (22.5 cm). Danske Tekniske Museum, Helsingør

The addition of some Latin verses lends these abstract cone anamorphoses an aura of erudition.

106, 107 Pieter Schenk (publisher). Individual graphics from a series of cone anamorphoses: *Man with a Wheelbarrow; Man with a Ladder; Two Men Boxing* (Plate 62); *Two Seashells* (Plate 54). Etchings, colored, 8¾ x 11¼″ (22.5 x 28.5 cm). Collection Elffers, Amsterdam; Universiteitsmuseum, Utrecht

In this series, particular attention was paid to the graphic effect of the reconstituted images. The *Man with a Ladder* is a geometric demonstration of the way to turn a curve into a straight line with the aid of a cone. The abstract compositions do precisely the opposite: The curving action of the cone permits the straight line to curve. The care with which the color combinations were chosen makes this one of the most beautiful series from the eighteenth century. With Series One there was a notation that more of these pictures, and mirrors, could be purchased in the shop of Schenk, "N. Vischers Atlas," in Warmoes Street in Amsterdam.

108, 109 Anonymous. Cone anamorphosis: *Skull*. Eighteenth century. Watercolor, 12 x 12″ (30.5 x 30.5 cm). Collection Elffers, Amsterdam

Here, too, the anamorphosis mirrors the relativity of the world.

*Fig. 34* Jean DuBreuil. *La Perspective pratique . . .* (Paris, 1649), pt. 3, p. 151

This engraving shows how to make a pyramid anamorphosis.

110–15  Anonymous (edited by V. Décugis). Perspective anamorphoses: *Napoleon III with His Children; A Woman Relieving Herself; An Eating Man with His Dog; Napoleon I; A Violinist; A Cellist.* 1868. Lithographs, colored

This series of lithographs not only brought the perspective type of anamorphosis back to life; the choice of themes can also be called "classic": genre scenes, royalty, obscenities.

116, 117  Ch. Hausman (editor). Perspective anamorphoses: *A Man Breaking Wind; Looking for Eggs.* c. 1840. Lithographs

118  Anonymous French. Perspective anamorphosis: *The Dog Rider.* c. 1810. Lithograph

119  J. W. Schwenck. Perspective anamorphosis: *A Castle.* c. 1870. Pen and wash drawing, 17¾ x 22″ (45 x 56 cm). Prentenkabinet, Leiden

The unique characteristics of perspective anamorphosis are used here in an unusual way. Seen from the correct angle, the entire drawing seems to leave the paper and stand out three-dimensionally.

120  Jan Dibbets. *Perspective Correction—My Studio II.* 1969

This photo, taken from an angle dictated by the construction of the square on the wall, is an artwork. The lines of wall and floor lead our eyes into the depth. The camera, pushing Alberti's perspective to its farthest limits, registers depth on the flat surface. Then, by drawing a square whose receding sides cancel the perspective reduction, Dibbets breaks through this perspective. It looks as though the square had been drawn on the photo *after* it was developed. The actual plane of the photo and the spatiality of Dibbets's studio confront each other. This anamorphosis in its most essential form is for Dibbets a means by which playfully to separate perception and reality.

121–25  Jan Beutener. "The Room," 1975

Seen through a peephole, the illusion of a normal scene is complete (Plate 121). Spectators can walk around the perimeter of the room without being seen from the peephole. When they do, they discover that except for the jacket, the light bulb, and the floor, everything is completely distorted. The real jacket, which seemed to be draped over the back of the chair (Plate 122), is really suspended on sharply angled wires (Plate 123), and the chair is only a painted triangle and a few pieces of wood lying on the floor. In Plate 124 the righthand wall and box are seen from another angle. Plate 125 shows the true construction of the box and the ladder.

126, 127  Nowadays anamorphoses still play a practical role. In traffic the Dutch are warned to drive thirty miles per hour, to stay in lane, and to use the bicycle path. To attract their attention, the relevant signs are painted in distorted fashion on the road. Seen from a distance, the signs, numbers, arrows, and bicycles regain their normal proportions.

Three cylindrical anamorphoses from China, now in private collections, are illustrated here (Plates 140–42). They are paintings on silk or paper, and a circle indicates the place where a reflecting cylinder is to be positioned. Experts date them as having been made between 1573 and 1619, a period when cylinder anamorphoses were unknown in Europe. They are loosely painted, which suggests that the artist looked in a cylinder while working on them.

Baltrušaitis has submitted the interesting hypothesis that Vouet saw the Chinese anamorphoses when he visited Constantinople on his way to Italy. Vouet joined the entourage of the French ambassador to the court of Sultan Ahmed I, who had a collection of Chinese *objets d'art*. From Constantinople, Vouet traveled to Rome and there drew some of the things he had seen.[5]

In France, anamorphoses for reflecting cylinders and cones quickly became established as part of the anamorphic repertoire. Simon Vouet, "*premier peintre*" to Louis XIII, designed the frontispiece for Niceron's *Thaumaturgus Opticus* of 1646. The frontispiece for *La Perspective curieuse* has also been attributed to him[6]; it shows a cylindrical anamorphosis of a portrait of Louis XIII.

An illustration of the principles of cylindrical anamorphic composition in *La Perspective curieuse* has as its model a picture by Vouet (Fig. 35). The painting itself is lost, but it originally hung in the monastery of the Minims in the Place Royale. Jean Lenfant made a copperplate engraving of it. The subject was once again St. Francis of Paola, this time in ecstasy. Vouet painted a number of scenes from the life of the saint for the monastery; unfortunately, they all disappeared during the French Revolution.[7]

In the Galleria Nazionale in Rome there is a series of four anamorphoses: a portrait of a couple; St. Francis of Paola in ecstasy; Louis XIII kneeling before a crucifix; and a portrait of Louis XIII (Plates 133–36).

In pose and dress, the portrait of the king (Plate 134) is very reminiscent of the picture of Louis XIII in the frontispiece of *La Perspective curieuse*. Probably it is modeled on one of the lost portraits of Louis by Vouet.

Another of these paintings is even closer to Vouet (Plate 134). At first, it appears as though Vouet's picture of St. Francis that Niceron copied had been used here as well. The shapes are by and large the same. Certain details, like the wrinkled brows and the rays fanning out over the head of Francis, however, are not in Niceron's illustration. They were taken from the original painting, as can be deduced by looking at the copperplate engraving by Lenfant.

This anamorphosis was thus probably made by an artist who had seen Vouet's painting with his own eyes. Niceron made the design ("*delineabat*") for the above-mentioned illustration in his book,[8] as the text accompanying the picture tells us. He also writes that he painted a composition of this sort, and that it was on view in the library of the Place Royale monastery. The proportions of the anamorphosis in Rome are indeed somewhat larger than those of the image in the book. An attribution to Niceron is further strengthened by the stylistic similarities between the portrait of Louis XIII and a so-called dioptric picture in Florence signed by Niceron. When one looks at this picture through a faceted lens, the painted Turks' heads shift into a portrait of Francesco de' Medici. These heads show the same sharply defined areas and strong light-and-dark contrasts.

The anamorphosis showing Louis XIII in his robes of office, kneeling before an altar with a crucifix on it while Fame holds his escutcheon (Plate 135), illustrates a virtue of the French monarchy—namely, royal piety.

The genre scene must have been derived from the work of a French follower of Caravaggio (Plate 133). This cycle may readily be associated with a particularly beautiful anamorphosis that recently came to Utrecht's Centraal Museum. At the museum it is thought that Matthias Stomer, a Dutch follower of Caravaggio and a member of the Utrecht School, executed it. The scene shows St. Jerome in prayer (Plate 128). The subtle effects of light and the naturalistic detailing of hands and faces are characteristic of Stomer's repertoire. He was in Rome at the beginning of the 1630s and so may have seen Niceron's paintings.[9] Yet the brushstrokes seem rather too loose for Stomer, who painted in smooth round forms. One of the French painters studying in Rome is a more likely attribution. Stylistic evaluations made in a mirror are not to be relied upon, however.

It is noteworthy that, at a very early stage, examples of anamorphic art appeared in the Netherlands, Germany, and Scandinavia.

The first example can be dated exactly. Moreover, it throws some light on the cultural context in which anamorphoses were seen in the seventeenth century.

Philipp Hainhofer, merchant and diplomat in the service of Duke Philipp II of Pomerania, came from Augsburg. Through his offices the city of Augsburg in 1632 bestowed upon King Gustavus Adolphus of

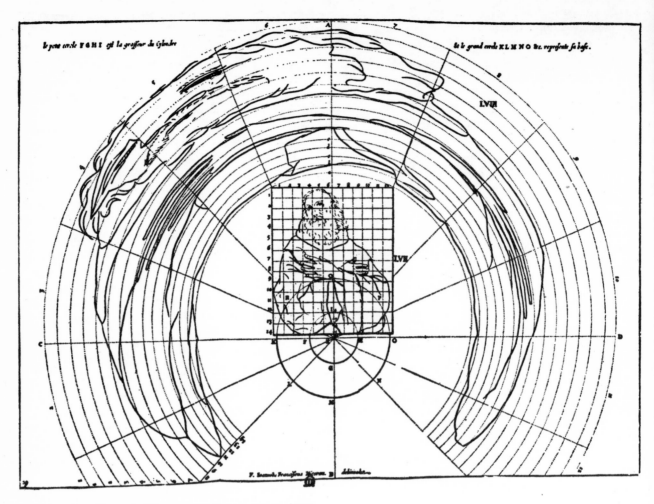

*Fig. 35* Jean-François Niceron. *La Perspective curieuse*
(Paris, 1638), illus. LVIII, LVII

Niceron uses a painting by Vouet as the model for this
illustration demonstrating how to make a cylinder
anamorphosis. Saint Francis of Paola, founder of his Order
and patron saint of the French royal house, again serves as
subject. An anamorphosis in Rome (Plate 134) is more
faithful to Vouet's painting than is this example.

Sweden a so-called *Kunstschrank*, or curio cabinet. This *Kunstschrank* is now in Uppsala. It is a piece of show furniture made of ebony and inlaid with cartouches painted on semiprecious stones. An arrangement of rare shells and corals crowns the lid. This cabinet contains a distorted painting on copper which is among the earliest examples of reflecting anamorphosis (Plate 150). The fact that Hainhofer bought oddly formed mirrors in Dresden in 1629 may be an indication that people were interested in reflecting anamorphoses before Vaulezard's book appeared in 1630.[10]

The light, enamel-like colors of the costume of the subject, who is depicted full length in front of a balustrade, are reminiscent of miniature painting. Johann König painted the cartouches on semiprecious stones and probably also painted the anamorphosis.[11]

Later in date is another anamorphosis in Scandinavia (Plate 139). It, too, was made by a German —Gerd Dittmers of Hamburg, in 1656. The painting, now in Copenhagen, was commissioned by King Frederick III of Denmark. He is portrayed together with his queen in a very secret way; without a cylinder, the composition is impossible to decipher.

Also in Copenhagen are the three perspective cabinets discussed earlier, in Chapter Six. The Danish court was apparently much intrigued by these odd perspective toys.[12]

Two anamorphoses, from the northern and southern Netherlands, take the Crucifixion as their theme. One of these, a particularly large and beautiful anamorphosis, shows, in severe distortion, a part of the famous *Raising of the Cross* that Rubens painted in 1610–11 as center panel of a triptych for the cathedral of Antwerp (Plate 130). Perhaps it is by one of his pupils. In order to eliminate the reflection of the cylinder, the painter added two inactive angel-spectators to the original composition.

Much more "conventional" is the Crucifixion showing Mary and St. John at the foot of the cross with angels rushing up (Plate 129). To judge by the technique, the painting was done by a north Netherlandish painter about 1640. The horizontal bands of the composition become, in the distortion, a striking system of curved, concentric elements.

At Castle Gripsholm near Stockholm is an anamorphosis that probably comes from England (Plates 131, 132). The composition takes a similar approach to the form that Holbein mastered in *The Ambassadors*. Mirrors are symbols of the superficial, illusory nature of the world, which is what we see. A portrait of King Charles I of England comes to life again in the mirror, but in the circle where the cylinder rests is a death's-head.

After the beheading of Charles I in 1649, Charles II succeeded—in theory. Power, however, remained exclusively in Oliver Cromwell's hands. Charles II is painted on the back of the same picture, decked out in the trappings of royal office. Resplendent in the circle is the imperial orb, which, until 1660, was to remain for him a meaningless object.

Notes

1  From the Greek *katoptron* (mirror).
2  L. Brion-Guerry, *Jean Pélérin Viator* (Paris, 1962), pp. 144–49.
3  G. Rodis-Lewis, "Machineries et perspectives curieuses dans leurs rapports avec le Cartésianisme," *Bulletin de la Société d'Etude du XVIIᵉ siècle* 32 (July, 1956): 461–74; J. Baltrušaitis, *Anamorphoses* (Paris, 1969), Chapter 5.
4  J. Baltrušaitis, *op. cit.*, pp. 151–52.
5  *Ibid.*, p. 173.
6  W. R. Crelly, *The Paintings of Simon Vouet* (New Haven and London, 1962), p. 16, n. 74.
7  *Ibid*, pp. 240–42.
8  J.-F. Niceron, *La Perspective curieuse* (Paris, 1638), pp. 83–88.
9  Cf. H. Pauwels, "De schilder Matthias Stomer," *Gentse Bijdragen tot de Kunstgeschiedenis* 14 (1953): 139–92.
10  H. Kreisel, *Die Kunst des deutschen Möbels* (Munich, 1968).
11  *Deutsche Maler und Zeichner des 17. Jahrhunderts*, exhibition catalogue (Berlin, 1966), illus. 151.
12  Poul Eller, *Kongelige portraetmalere i Danmark 1630–82* (Copenhagen, 1971), p. 238.

# 9. Popularization in the Eighteenth Century

During the next hundred years, cylinder and cone anamorphoses enjoyed great vogue and were no longer in the least recherché. Series of engravings appeared with the publisher's address printed on them. They could be produced in large quantities because craftsmen copied extensively from each other's works and worn-out plates could be reconditioned. One I. Leupold of Leipzig even designed a machine to draw anamorphoses, and there exists a series of engravings by his hand—if that expression can be justified in this context.[1] Engravings were also used as models for many gouaches during this period.

Anamorphic paintings were made, too, particularly toward the end of the century. They suddenly proliferated in England for a brief period, and in this regard the name of Henry Kettle is an important one. Until recently, we knew little about Kettle except that he was father of the well-known portrait painter Tilly Kettle, who lived from 1735 to 1786. Henry was a house painter, although it is also mentioned that Tilly studied art with his father. In 1772 Henry exhibited a "cylindrical painting" at the Society of Arts.

Two series of unsigned paintings (five cone and five cylinder anamorphoses) were purchased in 1939 by Herbert Tannebaum, an art dealer in Amsterdam (Plates 55–59, 151–55). Tannebaum emigrated to New York, and after his death a few years ago they were bought by the Roman art dealer Apolloni at auction. The latter sold most of them to a collector in Milan. Two were purchased by the photographer of this book, Michael Schuyt.

Among the cone anamorphoses is a hunting scene—a wild boar and its young attacked by a hunting dog (Plate 56).

The Rijksmuseum voor de Geschiedenis der Natuurwetenschappen in Leiden has two anamorphic paintings signed by Kettle. One is a pyramid anamorphosis. In the four corners are male portraits (Plate 97). When you place the reflecting pyramid that belongs to it in the center, a part of each of the four heads is mirrored, and together they form a new head. A similar pyramid anamorphosis was constructed earlier by DuBreuil (Fig. 34).

The other signed painting by Kettle in Leiden is a cylinder anamorphosis (Plate 155). It offers a clue to the author of the Tannebaum series, for it is extremely similar to the hunting scene just discussed (Plate 56) in the manner in which it is handled. Almost certainly, Henry Kettle rose from house painter to artist.[2]

Other names that are regularly mentioned in connection with anamorphic series in the eighteenth century are those of the Hertel publishing house in Augsburg (Plates 104, 105) and the Amsterdam publisher Pieter Schenk (Plates 62, 106, 107). The history of anamorphoses was now no longer one of ongoing discovery and invention. Anamorphsis had become a widely known phenomenon in which many people found enjoyment until the daguerreotype, which actually mirrored reality on its surface, satisfied even better the desire for strange and marvelous pictures.

Notes

1   J. Baltrušaitis, *Anamorphoses* (Paris, 1969), p. 160, fig. 122.

2   "Tilly Kettle," in *British Dictionary of National Biography*, vol. 31.

# Game Section

*To the plates on pages 137–76*

128 French follower of Caravaggio. Cylinder anamorphosis: *Saint Jerome Praying*. c. 1635. Oil on canvas, 16¾ x 23″ (42.4 x 58.5 cm). Centraal Museum, Utrecht

The chiaroscuro lighting and the "realistic" details make this anamorphosis unusually effective. This kind of representation was a favorite among French painters who were influenced by Caravaggio.

129 Anonymous north Netherlandish. Cylinder anamorphosis: *Crucifixion with Mary, John, and an Angel*. c. 1640. Oil on panel, 19⅝ x 24⅜″ (50 x 62 cm). Collection Elffers, Amsterdam (see Plate 100)

In the northern Netherlands there were, as we have learned from the perspective cabinets, many painters who were particularly interested in optical phenomena—clearly, a congenial atmosphere in which anamorphoses could originate.

130 Anonymous south Netherlandish. Cylinder anamorphosis: *Raising of the Cross*. First half of the seventeenth century. Oil on canvas, 24⅜ x 30¾″ (62 x 78 cm). Collection Rheims, Paris

This artist has used a portion of the famous Rubens painting (1610–11) in the Antwerp Cathedral and has added two angels.

131, 132 Anonymous English. Cylinder anamorphoses: *King Charles I of England* (front) and *King Charles II* (back). c. 1660. Oil on panel, 16⅛ x 19⅝″ (41 x 50 cm). Nationalmuseum, Stockholm

Charles I of England was beheaded in 1649, and, appropriately, a skull has been painted beneath his portrait in the circle where one places the cylinder. The fleeting nature of earthly existence, which the mirror suggests, is underscored by the symbol of death.

133 Jean-François Niceron. Cylinder anamorphosis: *A Couple*. c. 1635. Oil on canvas, 19⅝ x 26⅜″ (50 x 67 cm). Galleria Nazionale d'Arte Antica, Rome

This type of genre scene was popular among the French painters who were influenced by Caravaggio.

134 Jean-François Niceron. Cylinder anamorphosis: *Saint Francis of Paola*. c. 1635. Oil on canvas, 19⅝ x 26⅜″ (50 x 67 cm). Galleria Nazionale d'Arte Antica, Rome

135 Jean-François Niceron. Cylinder anamorphosis: *Louis XIII Kneeling Before a Crucifix, Above Him an Angel Bearing the King's Escutcheon*. c. 1635. Oil on canvas, 19⅝ x 26⅜″ (50 x 67 cm). Galleria Nazionale d'Arte Antica, Rome

The king's piety was part of the conception of French royalty.

136 Jean-François Niceron. Cylinder anamorphosis: *Portrait of Louis XIII*. c. 1635. Oil on canvas, 19⅝ x 26⅜″ (50 x 67 cm). Galleria Nazionale d'Arte Antica, Rome

137 Johann Heinrich Glaser. Cylinder anamorphosis: *Woman with a Jester*. c. 1650–60. Oil on panel, 15⅜ x 15⅜″ (39 x 39 cm). Historisches Museum, Basel

140–42 Anonymous Chinese. Cylinder anamorphoses: *Couples Making Love*. c. 1573–1619. Collection Jean Vlug, Brussels; Collection Charles Ratton, Paris; Collection Pardo, Paris

It is still not certain whether the cylinder anamorphosis was brought to China by the Jesuits or whether the Chinese discovered it for themselves. The themes seem to contradict the first possibility.

138 Johann Heinrich Glaser. Cylinder anamorphosis: *Portrait of a Mayor of Basel*. c. 1650–60. Oil on panel, 15⅜ x 15⅜″ (39 x 39 cm). Historisches Museum, Basel

Glaser was active not only in the area of perspective (see Fig. 26) but also in that of cylinder anamorphoses.

139 Gert Dittmers. Cylinder anamorphosis: *Double Portrait of King Frederick III and His Queen*. 1656. Oil on panel. Nationalmuseet, Copenhagen

This Hamburg painter has extraordinary mastery of the art of anamorphosis. The disguised form of this representation makes the work a true secret portrait.

143, 144 Anonymous. Cylinder anamorphoses: *Erotic Scenes*. Eighteenth century. Oil on canvas. Collection Charles Ratton, Paris

Since he had poor command of the technique, the painter was not able to conceal his delicate theme well.

145-48  Anonymous. Cylinder anamorphosis: *Crucifixion; An Angel with a Chalice and a Cross Appears to Christ; The Resurrection; Christ in His Tomb.* Eighteenth century. Gouache, 15 x 18½" (38 x 47 cm). Private collection, Milan

149  James Steere (?). Cylinder anamorphosis: *H.M.S. "Victory"*; in the circle: *Victory.* After 1786. Oil on panel, 17⅜ x 20⅞" (44 x 53 cm). Science Museum, London (see Plate 99)

150  Johann König (?). Cylinder anamorphosis: *Portrait of a Man Standing Before a Balustrade.* c. 1630. Universitätsmuseum, Uppsala
This early cylinder anamorphosis is part of a curio cabinet that Philipp Hainhofer arranged to have sent in 1632 as a gift from the city of Augsburg to King Gustavus Adolphus of Sweden. In this cabinet Gustavus Adolphus kept rare objects with which to entertain his guests.

151  Henry Kettle. Cylinder anamorphosis: *Sleeping Venus Uncovered by Amor.* c. 1770. Oil on panel, 14⅝ x 18⅞" (37 x 48 cm). Collection Schuyt, Amsterdam (see Plate 101)
In seventeenth-century French painting this erotic motif is frequent. This kind of theme lends itself naturally to concealed portrayal.

152  Henry Kettle. Cylinder anamorphosis: *Par Une Tendre Chansonette.* c. 1770. Oil on panel, 14⅝ x 18⅞" (37 x 48 cm). Private collection, Milan
In Cambridge there is a painting with the same theme and the same title by Lancret, a painter who was very popular in England at the time.

153  Henry Kettle. Cylinder anamorphosis: *Couple Making Music.* c. 1770. Oil on panel, 14⅝ x 18⅞" (37 x 48 cm). Private collection, Milan

154  Henry Kettle. Cylinder anamorphosis: *Still Life with a Monkey and a Dog.* c. 1770. 14⅝ x 18⅞" (37 x 48 cm). Private collection, Milan
This type of still life with quarreling monkeys belongs to the standard repertoire of seventeenth-century Flemish animal painters.

155  Henry Kettle. Cylinder anamorphosis: *A Wild Boar Defends Its Young Against a Dog.* c. 1770. Oil on panel, 10½ x 14⅝" (26.7 x 37 cm). Rijksmuseum voor de Geschiedenis der Natuurwetenschappen, Leiden (see Plate 56)

156  Anonymous Dutch. Cylinder anamorphosis: *A Woman Shows Herself from an Unusual Angle.* End of the eighteenth century. Pen and wash drawing. Collection Dreyfuss, Basel

157  Anonymous. Cylinder anamorphosis: *Vanitas Still Life.* Eighteenth century. Gouache, 14⅞ x 18" (37.6 x 45.6 cm). Collection Apolloni, Rome
The fact that the world mirrored in the cylinder is an illusion underscores the theme embodied by symbols of the transitory nature of life.

158  Anonymous Indian. Cylinder anamorphosis: *Peacock.* Nineteenth century (?). Paint on paper, 8⅝ x 8⅞" (22 x 28.5 cm). Collection Elffers, Amsterdam

159  Monogramist 🐝, Augsburg. Cylinder anamorphosis: *Pan Entices Diana with a Hank of Wool.* Second half of the eighteenth century. Etching, colored, diameter 16½" (42 cm). Collection Elffers, Amsterdam

160  Annibale Carraci. Ceiling painting, (detail): *Pan Entices Diana with a Hank of Wool.* 1597-1601. Gallery, Palazzo Farnese, Rome
Carraci's compositions set the standard for academic painting. His famous ceiling painting served as model for an anamorphosis (see Plate 159). The theme is taken from Virgil's *Georgics* (III, 393). The relevant lines were added to the representation in the graphic.

161, 162  Anonymous. Cylinder anamorphoses: *Male Head, Two Men Fighting.* Eighteenth century. Etchings, colored, 8¾ x 11⅛" (22.3 x 28.3 cm). Collection Elffers, Amsterdam

163  Anonymous Netherlandish. Cylinder anamorphosis: *A Three-Master.* Eighteenth century. Colored etching, 9⅝ x 14⅝" (24.4 x 37 cm). Collection Elffers, Amsterdam

164  Anonymous. Cylinder anamorphosis: *A Dog.* Eighteenth century. Colored etching, 8¾ x 11⅛" (22.3 x 28.3 cm). Collection Elffers, Amsterdam

165  Anonymous French. Cylinder anamorphosis: *A Ballerina.* Nineteenth century. Lithograph. Collection Elffers, Amsterdam

166  Anonymous. Cylinder anamorphosis: *A Buffoon.* Eighteenth century. Gouache. Collection Elffers, Amsterdam

167  Anonymous. Cylinder anamorphosis: *Dominoes.* Eighteenth century. Gouache, 7⅞ x 13¾" (20 x 35 cm). Museo di Storia della Scienza, Florence

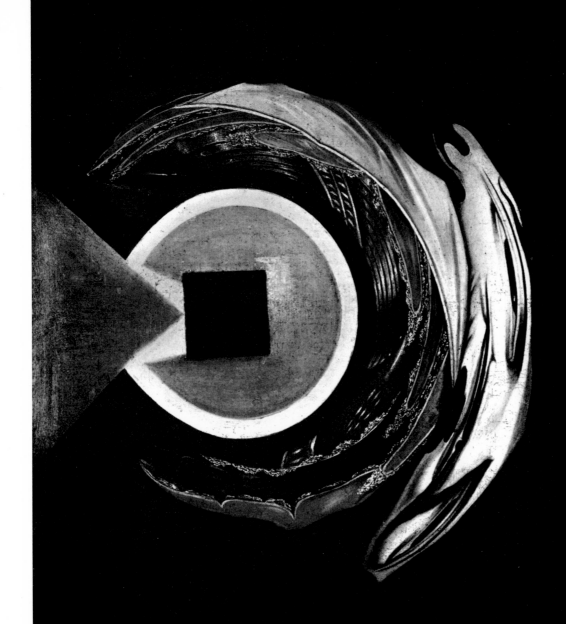

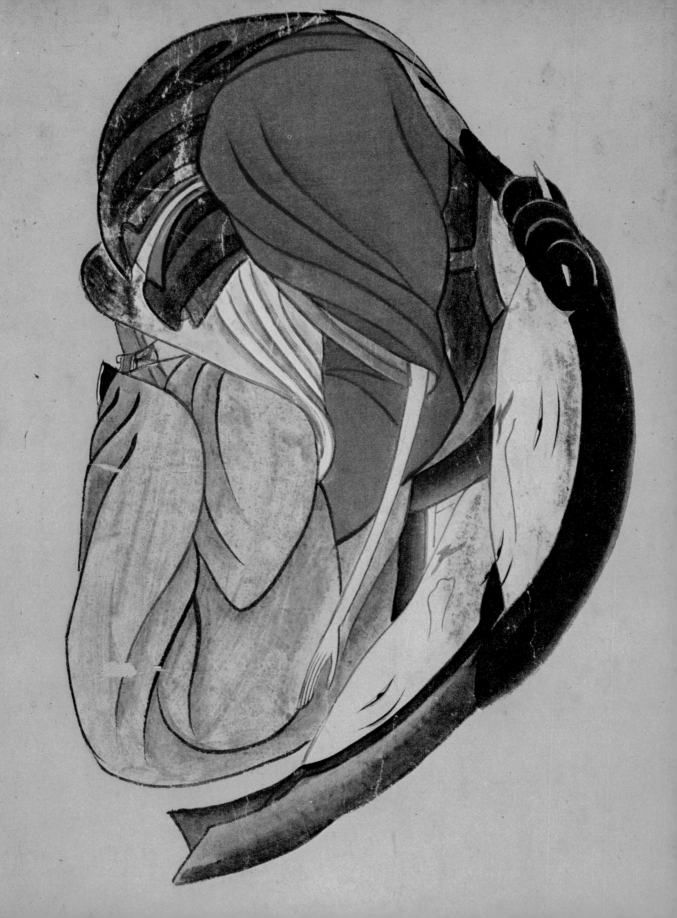

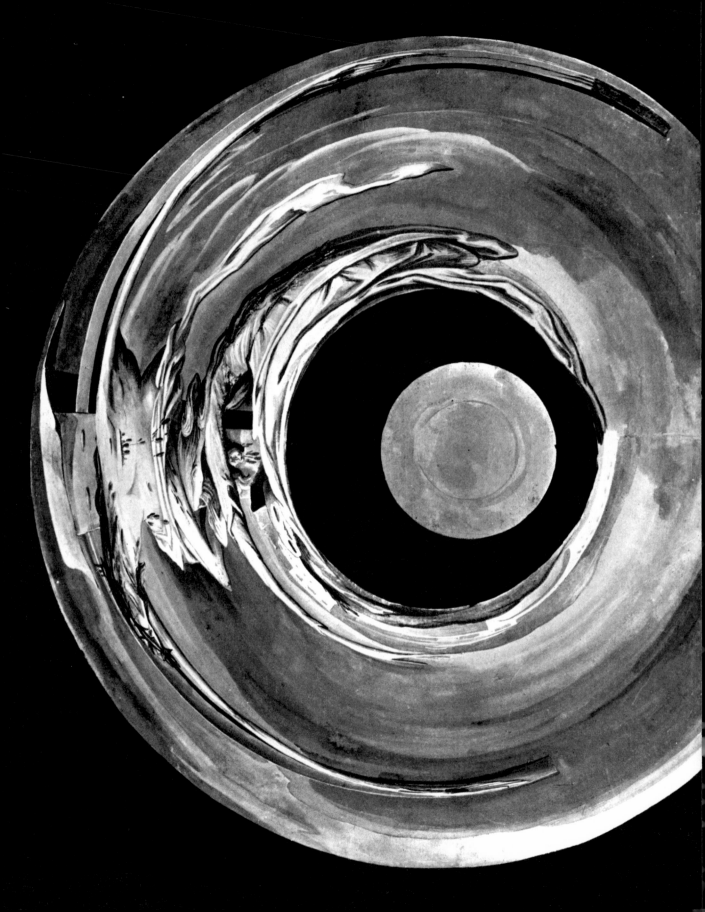

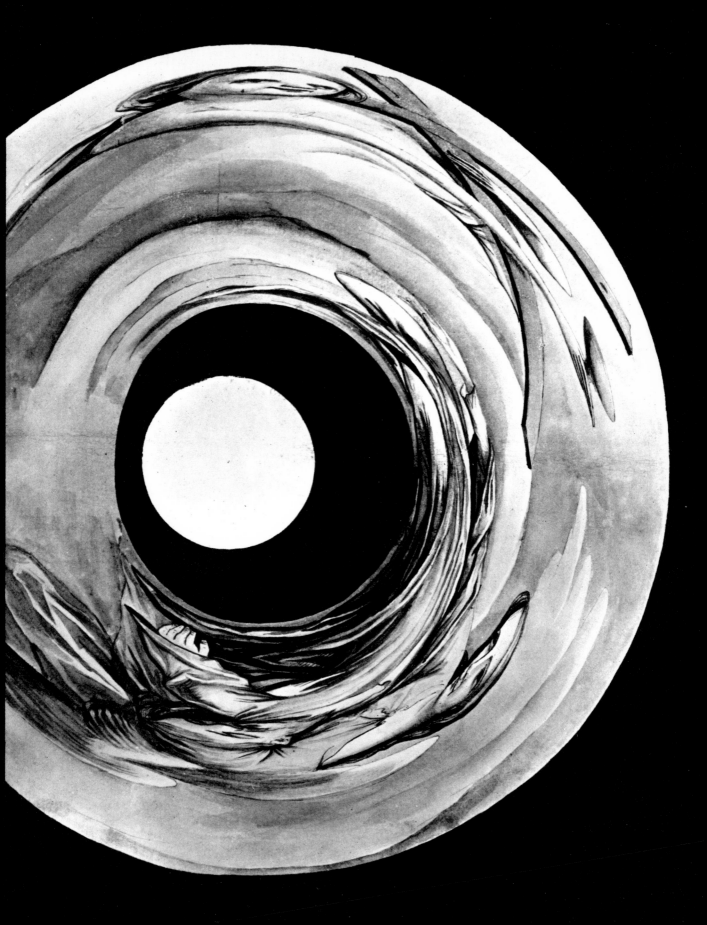

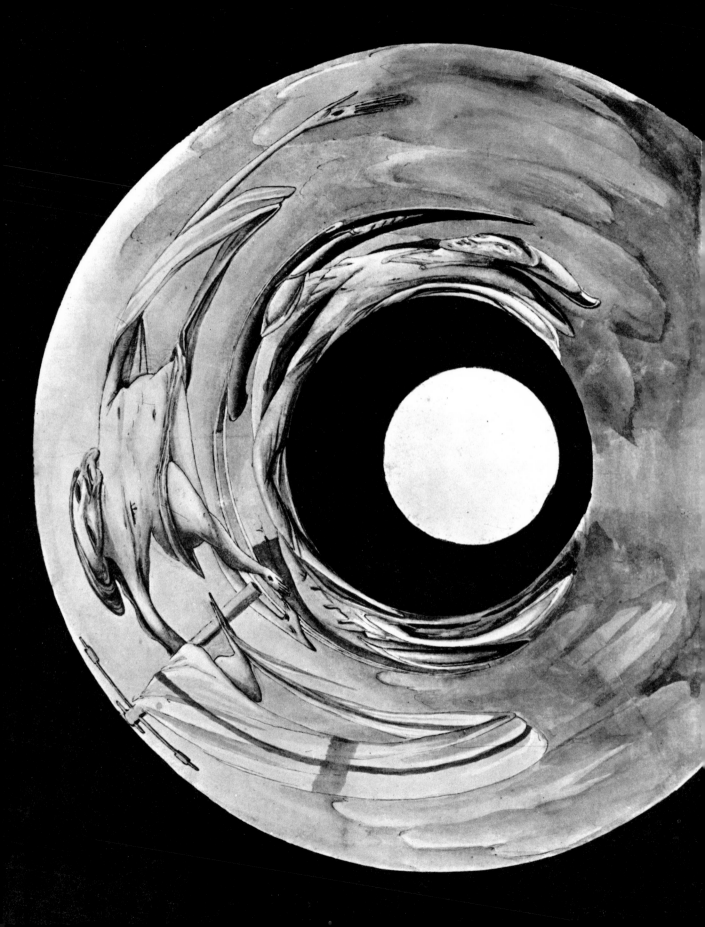

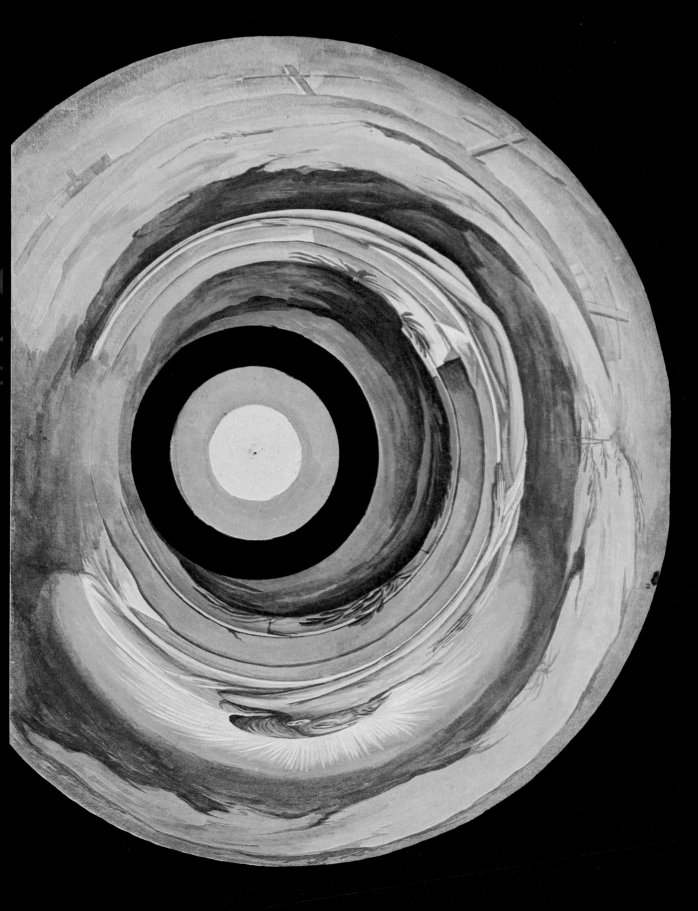

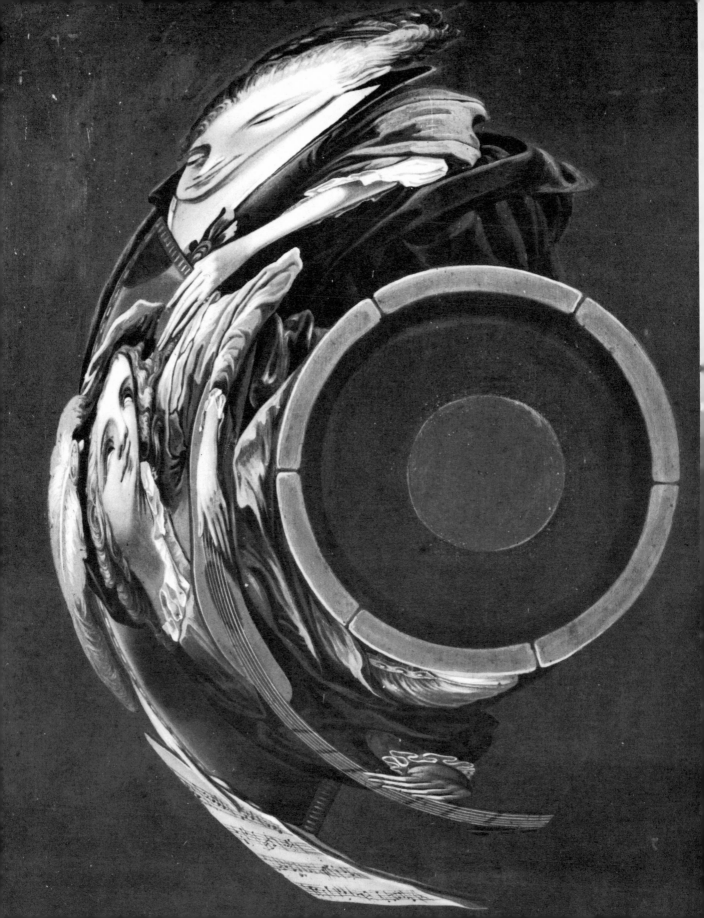

153

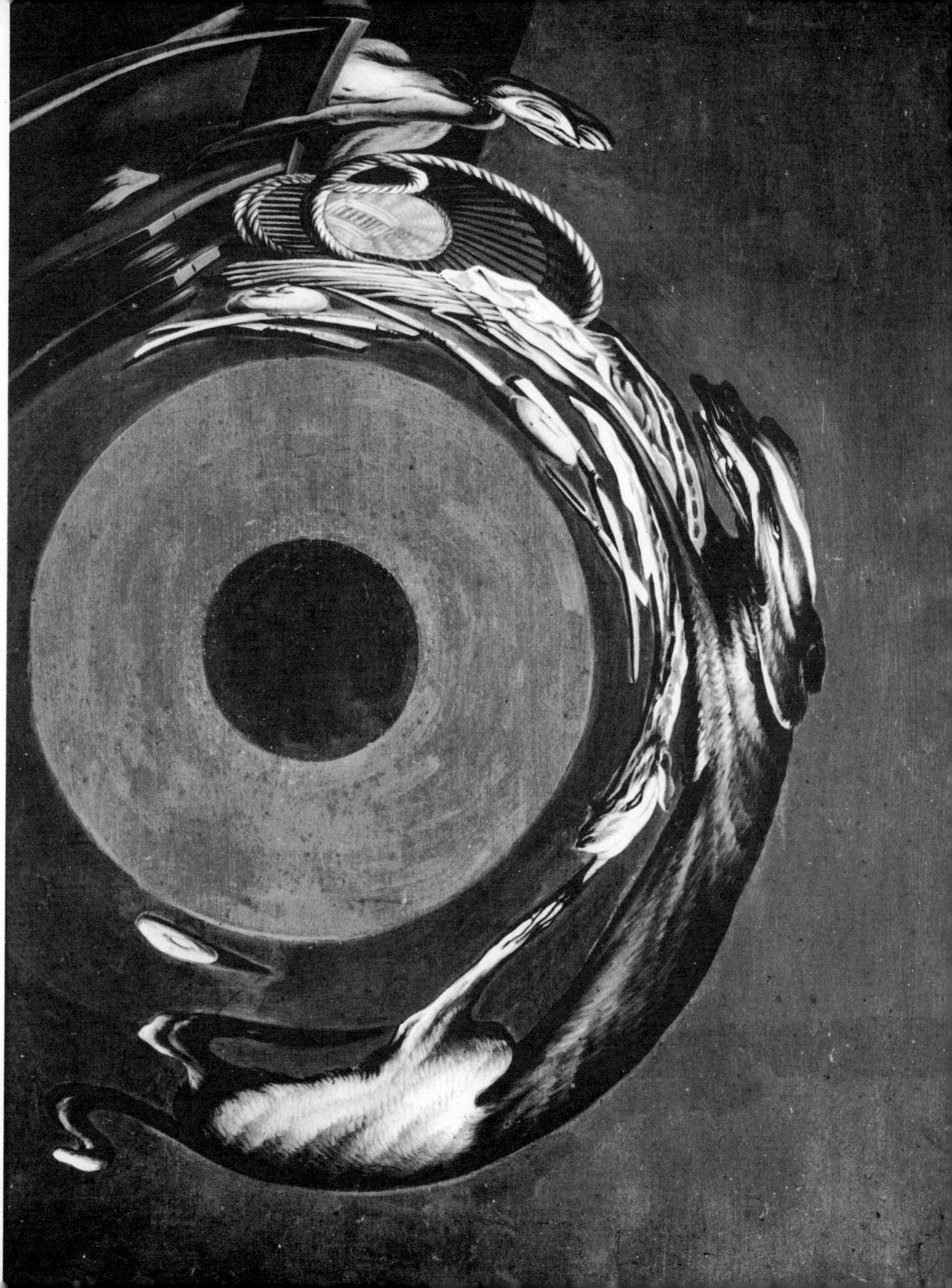

154

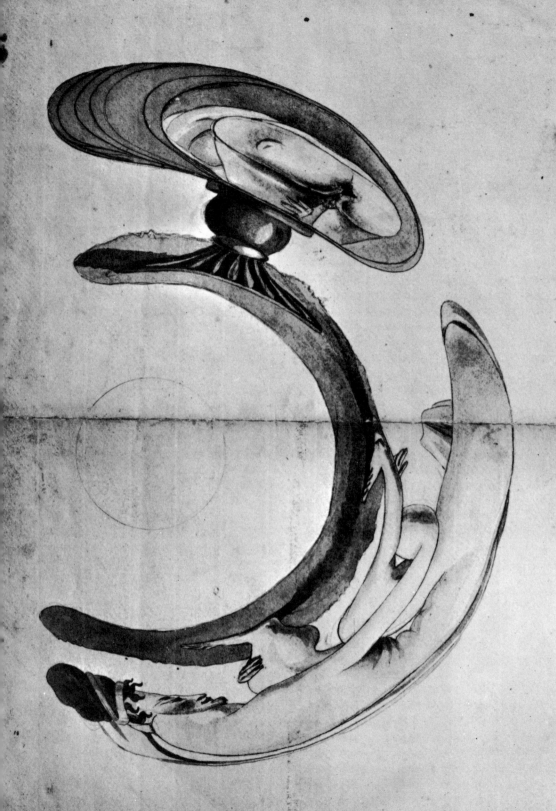

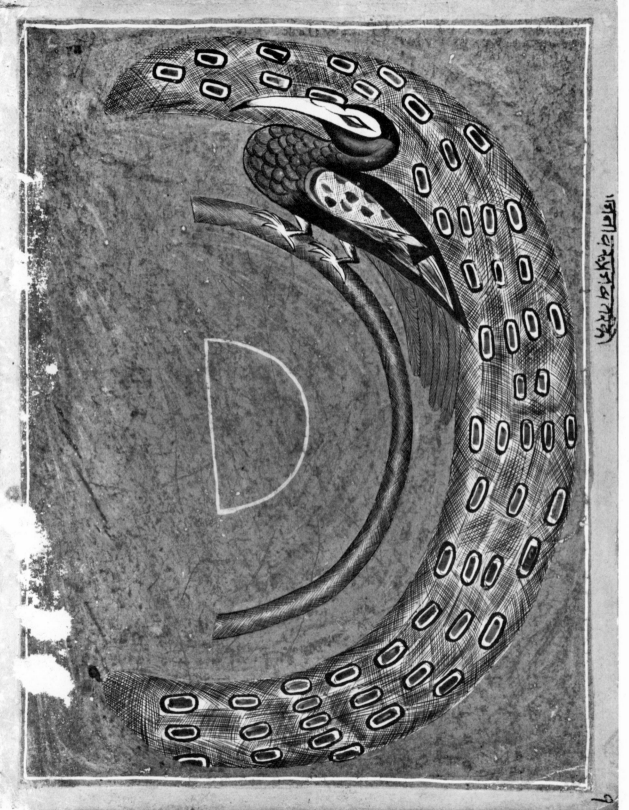

जानवरायापनवारकी

14.

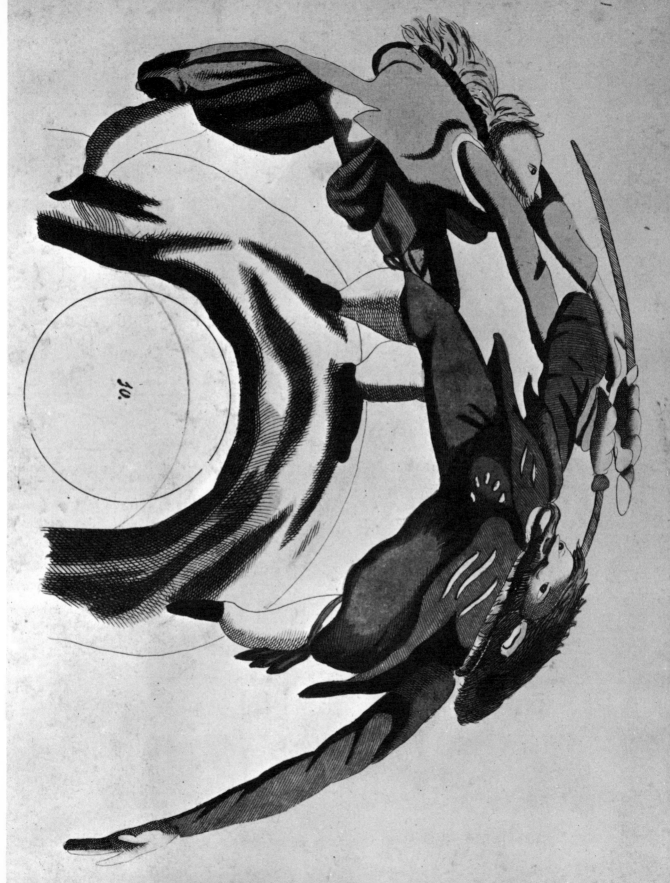

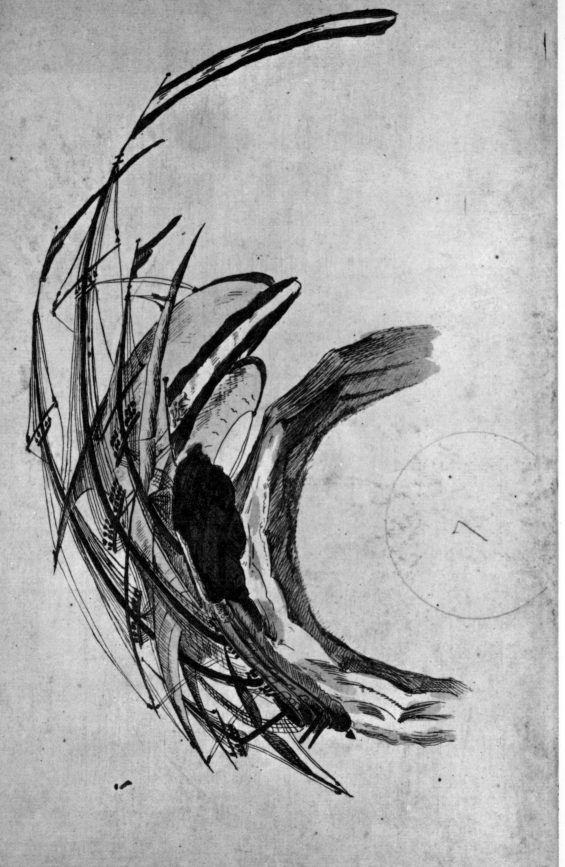

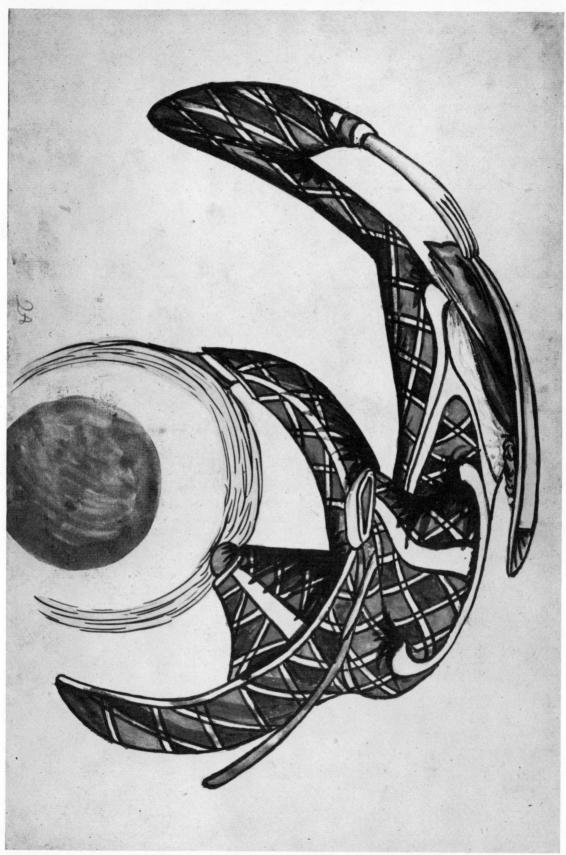

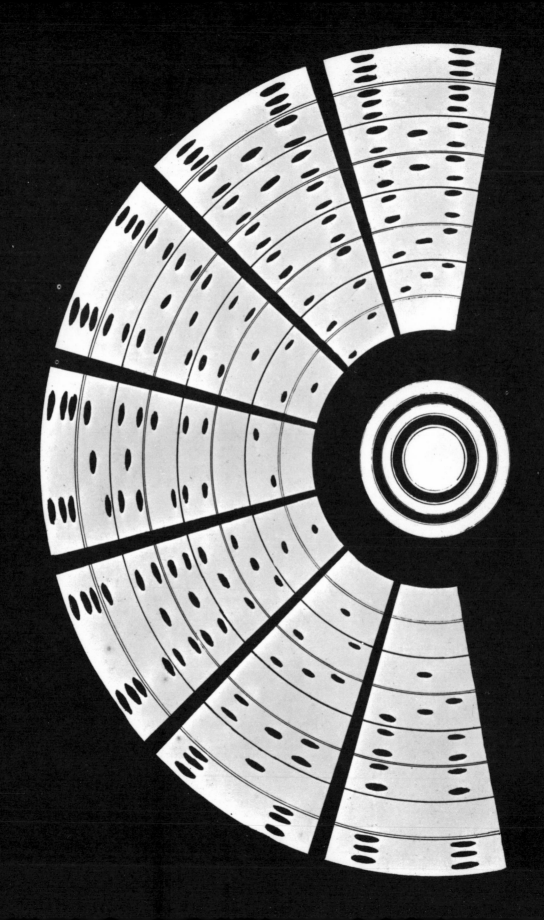